Bullitt

The Cars and People Behind Steve McQueen

CarTech®

MATT STONE

CarTech®

CarTech®, Inc.
6118 Main Street
North Branch, MN 55056
Phone: 651-277-1200 or 800-551-4754
Fax: 651-277-1203
www.cartechbooks.com

CarTech books may be purchased at a discounted rate in bulk for resale, events, corporate gifts, or educational purposes. Special editions may also be created to specification. For details, contact Special Sales at 6118 Main Street, North Branch, MN 55056 or by email at sales@cartechbooks.com.

© 2020 by Matt Stone

Edit by Bob Wilson
Layout by Connie DeFlorin

ISBN 978-1-61325-529-2
Item No. CT663

Library of Congress Cataloging-in-Publication Data

Names: Stone, Matthew L., 1958- author.
Title: Bullitt : the cars and people behind Steve McQueen / Matt Stone.
Description: Forest Lake, MN : CarTech, Inc., [2020]
Identifiers: LCCN 2020010163 | ISBN 9781613255292 (hardcover)
Subjects: LCSH: Bullitt (Motion picture)–Miscellanea. | McQueen, Steve, 1930-1980–Miscellanea. | Stage props. | Automobiles in motion pictures.
Classification: LCC PN1997.B7927 S86 2020 | DDC 791.43–dc23
LC record available at https://lccn.loc.gov/2020010163

Written, edited, and designed in the U.S.A.
Printed in China
10 9 8 7 6 5 4 3 2

Cover Art Credit:
David Pucciarelli
https://dave-pucciarelli.pixels.com/

Title Page Art Credit:
Nicolas Hunziker

Author note:
Many of the vintage photos in this book are of lower quality. They have been included because of their importance to telling the story.

DISTRIBUTION BY:

Europe
PGUK
63 Hatton Garden
London EC1N 8LE, England
Phone: 020 7061 1980 • Fax: 020 7242 3725
www.pguk.co.uk

Australia
Renniks Publications Ltd.
3/37-39 Green Street
Banksmeadow, NSW 2109, Australia
Phone: 2 9695 7055 • Fax: 2 9695 7355
www.renniks.com

Canada
Login Canada
300 Saulteaux Crescent
Winnipeg, MB, R3J 3T2 Canada
Phone: 800 665 1148 • Fax: 800 665 0103
www.lb.ca

Contents

DEDICATION

This marvelous studio publicity photo from 1968 shows Steve McQueen, the "King of Cool" indeed, in full Bullitt chase scene costume as well as his iconic Mustang. Here the car is parked in front of the building used to represent Lt. Frank Bullitt's apartment at 1153 Taylor Street. Notice the nice Austin-Healey 3000 parked just behind, and this appears to be the hero/beauty Mustang, serial number ending in 559, as it has no driver's side rearview mirror, which was removed to give the cameras a cleaner shot inside the driver's window. The other stunt/jumper Mustang is always seen with this door mirror in place. (Photo Courtesy ©/™ Warner Bros. Entertainment Inc. [sl9])

First and foremost, this book is dedicated to the incomparable Steve McQueen: the driving force (pun intended) behind everything that made *Bullitt* a success, both in 1968 and today, and by extension to Neile Adams McQueen. They both are Hollywood royalty of the first order. Additionally, to everyone else who acted in or otherwise worked on or contributed to this remarkable film.

And to Steve McQueen's grandchildren: Chase, Madison, Molly, and Steven R. McQueen (sadly Steve didn't live to

The Steve McQueen family is at home in Brentwood, California, aboard one of Steve's many big Triumphs. From left to right are Chad, Steve, Terry, and Neile. (Photo Courtesy McQueen Family Collection)

Two of the "new faces of McQueen" are Chad's son Chase (left) and daughter Madison (right) both aboard a 2019 Mustang Bullitt. Chase, a serious car guy, racer, and former professional soccer player, works in social media management, while Madison is an actress, model, painter, and fashion designer. (Photo Courtesy Ford Motor Company)

Actor Steven R. McQueen, with his father, Chad, check out a limited-edition Steve McQueen Triumph.

know any of them) who each bring a bit more of Steve McQueen's legacy and personality to life in the here and now.

Finally, to my friend Anthony Bologna, a certified *Bullitt*head who grew up and still lives in the San Francisco Bay area, the real and metaphorical home to Bullitt. Anthony was there as a young teen when it all happened and contributed tirelessly and unselfishly to this project. I thank you, buddy.

Our thanks and acknowledgments to Chad McQueen; Bob, Connie, Andrea, and everyone else at CarTech Books; Linda, Frank, Mel, Cathy Bertolette, and Irene Valdez at Warner Brothers Studios; Liz Van Denburg; Dave Green; Glen Kalmack; Kevin Marti; Ernest Nagamatsu; Galen Govier; Beau Boeckmann; Galpin Auto Sports; Ralph Garcia Jr.; Jeff Cater; David Pucciarelli; Raymond Smith; Sandi Troiano; the Boys Republic school; Steeda Performance; Christine Giovingo; Nicolas Hunziker; Mecum Auctions; and the Media Relations and Public Affairs Teams at Ford Motor Company.

Made in San Francisco: the original 1968 Bullitt Mustang hero/ beauty car used to make the film, the Golden Gate Bridge, and my friend Anthony Bologna. (Photo Courtesy Anthony Bologna)

FOREWORD
BY CHAD MCQUEEN

Chad McQueen is Steve and Neile Adams McQueen's only son, born December 28, 1960. After stints as an actor and producer, McQueen the younger enjoyed a successful career in sports car racing. He is father to three of Steve and Neile's grandchildren and is today a consummate automobile, motorcycle, and motorsport enthusiast.

"Hey, Dad! Watch this!" Steve McQueen hitches a ride with 10-year-old son Chad during the summer of 1970 on set for the filming of Le Mans **in France. Chad developed a love of two-wheeled machines early on and today owns several of his father's vintage bikes. (Photo Courtesy McQueen Family Collection)**

I was just a kid of 7 and 8 years old during the formative stages and pre-production development of *Bullitt,* so I don't remember a lot. I do recall my dad staying in San Francisco to make this film and that my mom visited him on set several times during the spring of 1968. My late sister Terry and I also went up to visit for a weekend or two.

I remember that he took delivery of a Ferrari 275/GTB 4-cam while up in the city during production. His Jaguar XK-SS was also shipped up to San Francisco for his use locally as was one of his favorite Triumph motorcycles, which fortunately I still have in my garage. Of critical importance to my dad was that the film embody as much absolute realism as possible. No

camera speed-ups or bullshit photography. The guys had to drive that chase scene in real time with real cars, and they were the best too: Bill Hickman, Carey Loftin, Bud Ekins (who was like an uncle to us), and my dad.

What a lot of people don't know is that he had visions of his epic racing film (which became *Le Mans* just a few years later) in his head already by then. Just a few years prior to *Bullitt,* and thus five to six years before he made his endurance racing classic *Le Mans* in 1970, a movie that involved fast car action and an immersive visual experience was already brewing in his mind, and this greatly impacted the way *Bullitt* looked and was filmed. He wanted not only reality but

Steve McQueen took delivery of this 1967 Ferrari 275 GTB/4 in San Francisco during the filming of Bullitt. Note that one of the Bullitt Mustangs is just visible at the right side of this frame with Steve looking fine in the full Lt. Bullitt chase scene costume. This Ferrari lived a fascinating life post McQueen, and at some point, it was professionally decapitated into a two-seat convertible. It was painted many colors during its long life. A subsequent owner located the previously removed roof panels, along with other parts, and shipped the car to the Ferrari factory in Maranello to be fully and comprehensively restored as a coupe and to otherwise original specifications. It was sold at public auction by RM Auctions in Monterey, California, in 2014 for over $10 million. (Photo Courtesy McQueen Family Collection)

Chad McQueen is at the wheel of a Ferrari 250GTL Lusso that was previously owned by his father. Note that like his father, he often wears his Rolex Submariner on his right wrist, even though he is right-handed. This Lusso was factory-painted a subtle metallic brown, so it was sexy, sporty, and elegant but didn't scream in over-the-top ways. Chad commented that "this looks absolutely like something my dad would have owned and driven."

Chad McQueen is pictured at the 2018 Fabulous Fords Forever car show in Buena Park, California, with one of the prototypes for the new 2019 Mustang Bullitt edition. As with all previous Bullitt edition Mustangs, serial number 1 was built with his name on it and destined for his own collection.

Chad is shown with his own Bullitt collection. At the left is a 2008 second-generation Ford Bullitt, in the middle is a 1968 Bullitt tribute built up on a new Dynacorn body/chassis for the automotive television series Rides, and at right is his 2001 Bullitt. Of course, the 2001 and the 2008 are the number 1 cars built of each series.

deep visual immersion—that feeling of really being there, in the car, in the seat, and in the scene. San Francisco was and remains a visually compelling city, and it lent itself to a crazy exciting car-chase scene. The majority of *Bullitt* was not filmed on a soundstage or a studio back lot, except for a few minutes of the opening office building scene that established the story's beginning in Chicago (which was shot on an L.A. soundstage) and the occasional fill-in or detail pick-up shot. The idea was a pit-of-your-stomach and visually brilliant backdrop that could be no place other than San Francisco. Near the end of production as the film was nearing its budget, the studios asked my dad to bring the production back to Los Angeles and finish it in SoCal, which of course my dad and director Peter Yates did not allow.

There are urban legends and rumors about how my dad and the team settled on the Mustang GT390 as Lt. Frank Bullitt's car of choice. Some speculate that my dad or Warner Brothers had a deal with Ford and had to use one. Again, BS. There's also speculation that they were considering a Shelby GT350 for *Bullitt*; more BS. They came to the Highland Green GT and that look because they felt it had the performance to make the cut in a high-speed chase scene, and my dad just felt that it looked like something an independent-minded guy like Frank Bullitt would drive. My dad also told me that the Mustang was something Lt. Bullitt could afford on a detective's salary. The *Bullitt* Mustang was modified with a slightly toned-down look that was devoid of chrome or a luxury interior and made a bit

louder than stock. True, but more important to me was all the suspension and chassis work they did to make that car handle the corners and punishment that it did—it turned out to be an inspired choice.

The goal with this book is to share the facts about the backstory of *Bullitt*: the cars, actors, script, chase, and the 50th anniversary of its making. Just as importantly, the lies, rumors, and urban legends that are constantly heard about this film are disproved.

I'm often asked if *Bullitt* was my favorite among my dad's films. It's hard to say, but it's certainly one of them—and so is *Le Mans*, or look at the great work he did in *The Sand Pebbles* and *Papillion*. He did something like 90 percent of the stunt driving in *Bullitt*, which is far more than some people are aware of or give him credit for and further demonstrated how physically proficient he was. He could drive or race any kind of car, shoot a gun, wrangle a horse, was a trained martial artist, and was a world-class motorcycle rider and racer.

The fact that *Bullitt* holds up so well today and is still so popular all around the world is testimony that it was in fact pretty damn great.

Chad McQueen
January 2020

INTRODUCTION

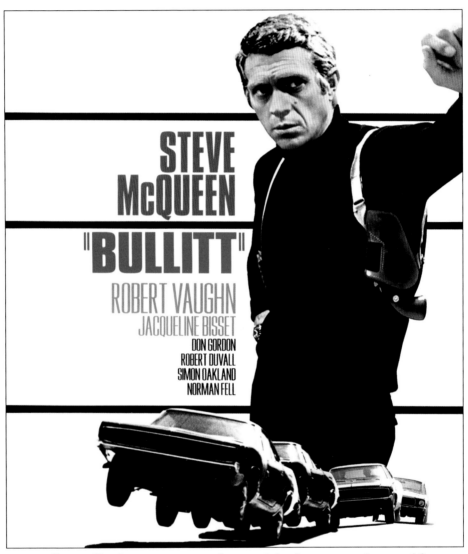

Even Bullitt's official movie poster referenced the famous car chase and featured McQueen's haunting look as well as Lt. Bullitt's under/over pistol holster, which was preferred by many detectives and FBI agents at the time for its quick-draw access and small bandolier of extra ammo housed under the right armpit. (Photo Courtesy ©/™ Warner Bros. Entertainment Inc. [sl9])

When the lists are made, the bets laid down, and the tallies taken, the 10 or so minutes of high-flying, crashing and burning, motorized mayhem between Frank Bullitt's High-land Green Metallic Mustang GT fastback and the bad guys' blacker-than-sin Dodge Charger R/T remains the best automotive chase scene ever filmed.

Utterly devoid of artifice (or spoken

There certainly isn't any question about which cast member or stunt driver is at the wheel for this famous burnout scene. Even though the Mustangs ran wider than stock tires front and rear, they were bias-ply rubber and had relatively good cornering grip but were slippery enough to make long, smoky burnouts easy enough. (Photo Courtesy ©/™ Warner Bros. Entertainment Inc. [sl9])

lines) but stacked full of action, great car sounds, and skilled and spectacular stunt driving, the *Bullitt* chase scene still stands tallest among the tall. That's not to say there hasn't been some great work done since *Bullitt* was filmed in early 1968. *The Seven-Ups, Vanishing Point, The French Connection, Ronin*, at least a couple of the Bourne films, and most recently *Baby Driver* have all included excellent chase scenes, and several of the directors who created them mention *Bullitt* as part of their inspiration.

This is among *Bullitt*'s many great mysteries: "What happened to the movie cars when filming wrapped?" That proved to be an evolving question. One of the two Mustangs used in the production was damaged badly in the final moments of the scene, and its intended future at the time was a date with the crusher followed by terminal meltdown. The other car was sold into private hands and then went into quiet hiding for decades. One of the Chargers was blown up in the explosive ending to the chase, while the fate of the second has been unclear for nearly as many years. Urban legend and the *Bullitt*sphere offered all sorts of answers and theories about the fate and whereabouts of these legendary movie cars, yet they seemed to all be founded in rumor and shrouded in enigma.

During 2017 and 2018, much of the picture became clearer. Both of the Mustangs used in the making of *Bullitt* sur-

In case you question Steve McQueen's chops as a serious car guy, check out this early 1970s McQueen family driveway roundup in Brentwood, California. At the bottom is Neile and her Excalibur, then Steve's favorite Jaguar XK-SS, their Ferrari 275/GTS, a C2 generation Corvette coupe, and a mildly customized 1968 Mustang notchback of unknown specification. (Photo Courtesy McQueen Family Collection)

The world-famous Cinerama Dome in Hollywood has been the site of countless memorable Hollywood premiere nights, and it was where I first saw Bullitt *in 1968. The tall, semiwraparound screen setup and excellent sound system made this theater the closest thing we had to an IMAX experience back in the day.*

faced. The car known to have survived and sold into private hands came out of hiding and was still owned by the family that bought it in the mid-1970s. The second car, far worse for wear, was hauled out of a guy's yard in Mexico. This coincided nicely with the golden anniversary for the making of the film.

I've written two previous books and countless magazine articles about Steve McQueen (as a car guy, motorcyclist, and racing actor, and the making of this defining film) all prior to the Mustangs surfacing. In deep discussions with the McQueen family, we decided that it was time to tell what we know and can determine, to dispel what we don't, and to properly celebrate 50 years of this cult-classic film.

It is unfortunate that so many of *Bullitt*'s star players are no longer with us: McQueen, of course; director Peter Yates; stunt coordinator Carey Loftin; stunt driver and double Bud Ekins; and cast members, including Don Gordon, Robert Vaughn, Norman Fell, Bill Hickman, and too many others. Some I was lucky enough to interview prior to their departure from the scene, and others have memorialized their thoughts and comments about the film and each other in a plethora of interviews, videos, and magazine articles.

I was 10 years old when *Bullitt* was new in theaters. My father took me to see the movie at the Cinerama Dome Theater in Hollywood. This is a famous and landmark place in Hollywood cinematic history. It was a sort of cinema in the half-round. The dome-shaped building allowed for very high ceilings and tall screens. Plus, it had what for the day was spectacular sound; it was as close to IMAX as we could have back then. Countless significant films made their Hollywood premiere at the Dome. I will never forget that I felt a bit woozy during those dramatic in-car shots as the Mustang was careening down those impossibly hilly streets in San Francisco. That's how legit the cinematography was and how fast those guys were driving as the cars bounced their way down those streets with oil pans smacking the asphalt and drivers banging those 4-speed transmissions and laying down those impossibly long burnouts. It made quite an impression on this car-crazy 10-year-old boy—one that lasts to this day.

Prior to reading this book, you'll get a lot more out of it if you watch *Bullitt* beforehand. Then, when you're done reading, watch the film again and you'll understand both a lot better. Let's head to San Francisco, wind the clock back five decades, jam the car into first gear, and punch it.

Thank you, and enjoy.

Matt Stone
January 2020

Chapter 1

LOADING THE BULLITT
THE BOOK OF A DIFFERENT NAME, IDEAS BEHIND MAKING THE FILM, AND PRODUCERS, CAST, CREW, AND LOCATIONS

Here Lt. Bullitt parks and exits the Mustang to visit a car wash where the cabbie portrayed by Robert Duvall, who transported Mafia witness Johnny Ross around town, has stopped for a wash and a smoke. This is in a grocery store parking lot just across the street from the car wash. This scene takes place just as the chase scene is beginning to form, and the bad guys' Charger and Bullitt's Mustang begin hunting each other just prior to the chase really breaking loose. (Photo Courtesy ©/™ Warner Bros. Entertainment Inc. [sl9])

Steve McQueen's rise to mid-1960s superstardom wasn't hot, it was meteoric. He turned in some worthy movie performances in the 1950s, yet American television audiences came to know and fall in love with him primarily for his leading role performance as bounty hunter Josh Randall in the series *Wanted: Dead or Alive*. The series first aired on television from 1958 to 1961, and McQueen starred in more than 90 episodes of that Western action/drama series. Just as *Wanted* was coming to a close, McQueen strung together a series of breakout movie roles that really put him on the world map of the most popular and highly paid actors. Those films included *The Magnificent Seven* (1960), where he first teamed up with longtime pal and costar Robert Vaughn and magically upstaged *Seven*'s headline star Yul Brynner; *The Great Escape* (1963), where not only his acting chops but his considerable talent as a motorcyclist shone brightly; *The Cincinnati Kid* (1965), where

Facing page: Even by 1968 and the filming of Bullitt, it would be impossible to know or count how many magazine covers Steve McQueen had appeared on. This wonderful cover indelibly casts the Steve McQueen look of Bullitt: the sharp haircut, the Persol shades, the Lt. Bullitt dress/casual outfit, the iconic Highland Green Metallic Mustang, and the San Francisco tableau in the background. This shot has it all, save for the burnouts and explosions.

AN AVON MYSTERY / G1293 / 50¢

MUTE WITNESS

ROBERT L. PIKE

Hell breaks loose in the Syndicate when a guy who talked too much is put out of commission

"FAST-PACED" Best Sellers

The original paperback cover of Mute Witness, *which was the genesis of the* Bullitt *story and screenplay. Note the cover price at the top: just 50 cents.*

he gave a commanding performance aside acting stalwart Edward G. Robinson; and most notably *The Sand Pebbles* (1966), in which McQueen delivered what many consider his finest-ever acting performance and earned him his only Oscar nomination for best performance by an actor in a leading role, which sadly he did not win.

By the time *Bullitt* was in the development stages in 1967, McQueen's star was white hot. His stature, popularity, unmitigated sex appeal, and box office bankability was fully the measure of the world's leading men.

Another factor that led to *Bullitt* becoming what he wanted it to be was that Steve McQueen formed his own film production company in 1960. It was originally called Condor Productions, but according to Neile McQueen, it later changed to Solar Productions. The marketing team felt it had more pizzazz, and it was the name of the Hollywood Hills street where the McQueens lived at the time. Steve wanted more creative control over the content and makeup of the films he produced and starred in. It was particularly important when his character was to be at the wheel of a car or aboard a motorcycle.

Most Hollywood studios viewed motorized exploits as a dangerous activity that risked injury or death to their star. As an active car and motorcycle racer, Steve ran afoul of studio legal departments in the past that told him what he could and couldn't do with cars and bikes. This posture isn't difficult to understand, but with McQueen as the boss, he had only himself and his financiers (more likely only the former) to be accountable to when it came to him running a race or driving his own stunt scenes.

In 1966 and 1967, McQueen and his Solar Productions executive producer Robert Relyea were looking for books that could be adapted into winning films. They

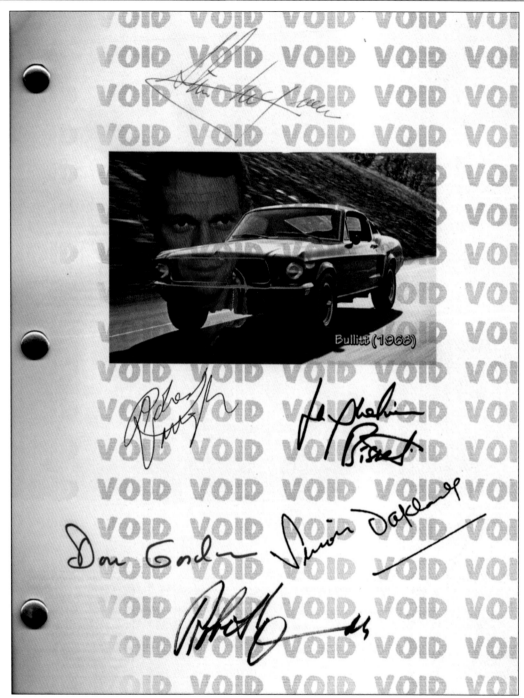

Bullitt (1968)

The cover of this reproduction copy of the original script was signed by several of the main cast members, including McQueen, Robert Vaughn, Jacqueline Bisset, Don Gordon, and Robert Duvall.

came upon *Mute Witness*, written and published by Robert L. Fish, who wrote under the name Robert Lloyd Pike, in 1963. In it,

they saw the bones of a potentially great film. When books are adapted into films, they often change considerably.

There is not a police detective character named Frank Bullitt in *Mute Witness*, and the book is set in 1950s Manhattan, not the late 1960s in San Francisco, California. And there's certainly no car chase between a Mustang and Dodge Charger;

San Francisco's unique architecture makes the perfect background for Bullitt. It looked, and still does today, like no other city in the world, could never be duplicated on a studio back lot, and offered the steep hills that made the ultimate chase scene so memorable. (Photo Courtesy ©/™ Warner Bros. Entertainment Inc. [sl9]; Alamy Stock Photos)

neither car had hit the market when *Mute Witness* was written.

Beyond that, a substantial amount of the original *Mute Witness* storyline became the footprint for *Bullitt*. There's a self-aggrandizing politician named Walter Chalmers who is hot on the trail of organized crime, and it also contains the plotline of a crime boss witness who is substituted for a hapless lookalike prior to his date to testify in court against the mob. Murder and mayhem abound in between,

and anyone with interest in the DNA of *Bullitt* must read *Mute Witness*. Paperback copies are often available at used book stores or on eBay to help clarify where the building blocks of *Bullitt* came from.

Solar bought the rights to *Mute Witness* and engaged Alan R. Trustman and Harry Kleiner to write the *Bullitt* screenplay. Trustman, an attorney who became deeply involved in screenwriting and ultimately retired from his law practice, is also significant in the McQueenosphere because he

Never question that Steve McQueen took a hands-on interest in how this movie was directed, filmed, and looked. Even though he never was credited as an assistant director, he somewhat filled that function by default. (Photo Courtesy ©/™ Warner Bros. Entertainment Inc. [sI9]; Alamy Stock Photos)

wrote the screenplay for McQueen's other 1968 smash hit film, *The Thomas Crown Affair*. Trustman also wrote the seminal Sidney Poitier film *They Call Me Mr. Tibbs*, so he clearly had screenwriting chops. Trustman read *Mute Witness* and adapted it into the *Bullitt* screenplay in just 20 hours. The primary producer of this Solar/Warner/Seven Arts joint venture was Philip D'Antoni.

Solar Productions partnered with Warner Brothers and Seven Arts Pictures to produce *Bullitt*, and Warner and Seven were set to distribute the film. Steve McQueen had visited San Francisco and had long felt it the ideal location for a great film, so he decided that his movie version of *Mute Witness* should be set there. His initial approach to the city was mildly rebuffed. One can only imagine the city's first response: "Excuse us, Mr. McQueen. You're saying you want to shoot a film with a high-speed car chase throughout the city, featuring a fiery explosion in its final scene?" But once Mayor Joseph Alioto got involved, the doors swung open more widely, as Alioto recognized the promotional benefits that a major Hollywood film starring Steve McQueen could offer his city in terms of attractiveness to travel, tourism, and business. Once Mayor Alioto established that McQueen and company were welcome, the terms were relatively simple. The production payed a $1 rental fee for "use of the city" in addition to the cost of police and fire protection and road blocking. Plus, the production payed for any damages caused by the filming. Additionally, McQueen donated the funds to build a much-needed swimming pool and recreation complex for the local Boys & Girls Club. Imagine those terms today, when it would surely cost millions of dollars and take years of negotiations to finalize.

Steve McQueen and director Peter Yates developed a great relationship and worked magic on the look and feel of the entire production of Bullitt, not just the chase scene. Yates was an inspired choice for the director's role and was hand-picked by McQueen because of his experience with on-location action sequences. (Photo Courtesy ©/™ Warner Bros. Entertainment Inc. [sl9]; Alamy Stock Photos)

Blue eyes and sunglasses; Steve McQueen and Jacqueline Bisset proved a perfect match in Bullitt. She was beautiful without being over the top, and the on-screen chemistry between the two stars came off as very genuine. (Photo Courtesy ©/™ Warner Bros. Entertainment Inc. [sl9])

This is from one of the many confrontational scenes between old friends McQueen (Lt. Bullitt) and Robert Vaughn (Chalmers). Another outstanding case of great cast member chemistry, the plain-talking Bullitt and the slithery Chalmers clash nonstop throughout the film, and it's clear that Vaughn and McQueen feel comfortable pushing each other to disagree. It is interesting that Robert Vaughn had some interest in a political career, but enough of his supporters felt that if he came off negatively as a politician in this performance it might actually diminish his appeal and likeability as a real-life politician. (Photo Courtesy ©/™ Warner Bros. Entertainment Inc. [sl9])

Even though Steve McQueen wasn't technically the film's producer, director, stunt coordinator, or director of photography, make no mistake that he was a dominant creative influence over what his leading role character would do and what plot elements the film would contain. It was he who divined that *Bullitt* would contain a pulse-pounding, over the top yet realistic car chase scene between his good guy, Lt. Frank Bullitt, and the mafia bad guys. There was no such scene in the book *Mute Witness*, but if the principal of Solar Productions said the film version would have one, then *Bullitt* would have it.

Critical, of course, was the choice of director. McQueen had seen and admired the work of British director Peter Yates, who was known for his masterful direction of action scenes, particularly those involving automobiles. Yates' first feature film as a director was *Summer Holiday* (1963). Subsequently, Yates directed various action and spy-related television episodes, including *The Saint* and *Danger Man*, showing a particular prowess for action sequences.

Another big feature film with Yates as director was the caper flick *Robbery* (1967), another spin on the original *Great Train Robbery*. *Robbery* was a critical success in the US. Upon meeting Yates, McQueen reputedly told him, "You're going to direct my movie!" So, Yates it was, and it ultimately proved to be a brilliant choice for everyone. Yates is most often lauded for *Bullitt*, and the film was certainly better for his involvement. He ultimately left his native England to move to New York to put him closer to larger movie offerings.

The *Bullitt* cast and crew were an amalgam of then-newer talent and some of McQueen's well-known and long-trusted friends and previous costars. British actress Jacqueline Bisset had only launched her movie career three years prior to the 1968 production of *Bullitt*, so she was a relative newcomer to American audiences. Cultured and a classic beauty with sparkling blue eyes like McQueen, Ms. Bisset was the perfect foil to McQueen's macho and handsome yet gritty homicide cop character. No matter if they posed together for studio PR still shots or showed up at a murder scene in the film, they made an unimaginably beautiful couple. The morning scene of her in Bullitt's apartment

Critical players in this hotel room scene include Steve McQueen as Lt. Bullitt (left), Felice Orlandi as the Albert Renick version of mafia money man Johnny Ross (middle), and Don Gordon as Lt. Delgetti (right). Gordon and McQueen were longtime personal friends apart from this

casting. (Photo Courtesy ©/™ Warner Bros. Entertainment Inc. [sl9])

You can bet that detailed aspects of the chase scene were being planned at this moment with director Peter Yates (left), car builder and camera car driver Max Balchowsky (back to camera), McQueen (making hand gestures so typical of racing drivers), and stunt coordinator/driver Carey Loftin (right). Note the interested onlookers in the background, among them young Joe Faccenda standing in the back row, far right, in a leather jacket, right hand in pocket. He stumbled, literally and figuratively, onto the set. His remembrances are in the epilogue. (Photo Courtesy ©/™ Warner Bros. Entertainment Inc. [sl9])

None of these kids are teenager Joe Faccenda, but no matter. Steve McQueen loved kids and always made time for engaging young kids who either seemed switched on and interested in what he was doing or needed some help. Notice the young man at right, camera raised, and the boy to his left who appears to be proffering something for McQueen to autograph. Having an international movie star and a big game movie production come to your town was very big stuff in the pre-Instagram era of 1968. (Photo Courtesy ©/™ Warner Bros. Entertainment Inc. [sl9])

Bud Ekins (left) and Steve McQueen (middle, wearing goggles) were friends, racing teammates, desert racing buddies, and stunt double and actor. Ekins was McQueen's motorcycle muse and got him actively involved in motorcycling and off-road racing. Ekins was already a motorcycle racing legend upon meeting McQueen, who bought all or nearly all of his bikes from Ekins' San Fernando Valley, California, motorcycle shop. This Petersen Automotive Museum exhibit display shows several of McQueen's off-road racing bikes, with a Husqvarna in the foreground and a pair of Triumphs behind.

wearing only a long-sleeved dress shirt is sexy beyond words without being blatant or risqué. Even with only a few years of top-level movie acting on her resume, she had more than enough chops to keep up with the powerhouse McQueen.

Besides the script's mafia hitmen characters, *Bullitt*'s other villain was ably portrayed by longtime friend and previous costar Robert Vaughn. Sophisticated and uber handsome, Vaughn was cast as the career-driven politician/prosecutor Walter Chalmers, who was looking primarily to further his own career. The name and character carried over quite faithfully from *Mute Witness*. Vaughn gave Chalmers an eerie, slithery demeanor that clashed with McQueen's Bullitt's straightforward, result-driven methods and personality. The tension between them was palpable.

Vaughn later said at the screening that he felt the plot was "really complicated and in some places difficult to follow, yet McQueen could be most persuasive, and the more zeroes they kept adding to his compensation offer, the better I liked the script."

Detective Delgetti, ably played by Don Gordon, was another McQueen crony. They were friends and had met and worked together on a few episodes of *Wanted: Dead or Alive*. Gordon once told me that "nobody worked harder on set than McQueen. He worked very hard to overcome his dyslexia and was a complete perfectionist. Yet when he and I would go out riding motorcycles around San Francisco, he was a ton of fun."

Another interesting yet not entirely surprising casting choice was that of Rat

Bill Hickman was an actor who could play a dozen different characters depending on hair, costume and makeup. Give him longish straggly hair and dirty clothes, and he's a drug dealer. Put him in uniform, and he's a clean-cut soldier. In this case, wrap him in a pinned-down-looking black suit, and a pair of "Harvard Law Professor" glasses, and he's a menacing, wordless Mafia hitman's assistant. No matter the dress, he was a wicked good stunt and precision driver, considered by many to be the best of his era. Hickman and McQueen spent a lot of time trading paint in Bullitt. (Photo Courtesy McQueen Family Collection, © and ™ Warner Bros. Entertainment Inc. [sl9])

Packer Norman Fell, who played Frank Bullitt's senior most police captain. Fell was a popular movie and television actor in the 1960s and 1970s, and *Bullitt* was his first on-screen credit with McQueen.

Simon Oakland, who appeared in several McQueen films over time, also played San Francisco Police Department (SFPD) Captain Sam Bennett. Grayish-blond character actor Paul Genge is identified as Mike the hitman. Bill Hickman played Phil, the hitman's partner and driver, whom we'll talk about in future chapters. Two different but similar-looking actors played the central Mafia witness Johnny Ross. Felice Orlandi was Albert "Johnny Ross" Renick, and Pat Renella was the *real* Johnny Ross. Robert Duvall played a generally humble cab driver who ferried Lt. Bullitt around town a few times and also provided a few critical bits of information about the movements of Johnny Ross.

Critically important were a roster of more behind the scenes casting choices. To help plan, orchestrate, and direct the seminal car chase scene, Yates and McQueen chose Carey Loftin (January 31, 1914–March 4, 1997). At the time, Loftin was among Hollywood's very best stunt

men, vehicle stunt drivers, and action stunt coordinators. He continued his successful career for more than six decades. Many experts rank him as one of the film industry's most accomplished stunt drivers because he focused on stunt safety as well as spectacular action. His body of work included classic films such as Steven Spielberg's *Duel*, *Thunder Road*, *Bullitt*, *Vanishing Point*, and *The French Connection*.

Bud Ekins is the stuff of motorcycle racing and stunt riding/driving legend. He was also among McQueen's closest friends and without question his primary motorcycling muse. McQueen spent considerable time hanging out at Ekins' San Fernando Valley motorcycle shop. The two cranked on bikes all the time and spent countless days and weekends racing and riding bikes in the Southern California deserts. Bud and Steve, along with Bud's brother Dave and another Hollywood stunt-type named Cliff Coleman, teamed up to represent the United States in the exceedingly difficult International Six Day Trial motorcycle endurance event in (then) East Germany in 1964. It was also Ekins who rode the famous motorcycle fence jump stunt in *The Great Escape*. Ekins and McQueen

Steely-eyed character actor Paul Genge played "Mike" the mafia hitman sent by the organization in Chicago to take out the witness, Johnny Ross, that Lt. Bullitt was assigned to protect. You'll note that Mike and his Winchester pump shotgun were pressed close up against the doorframe of the black Dodge Charger as the mafia hit pair, having successfully killed the stand-in for Ross, are now after Lt. Bullitt near the end of the chase scene. Genge was handsome enough to have played your uncle or grandfather yet creepy enough to be a mafia hitman. (Photo Courtesy ©/™ Warner Bros. Entertainment Inc. [sl9]; Alamy Stock Photos)

were about the same size and had similar features, so Bud was a natural stunt double for the *Bullitt* star. Bud was roped into the *Bullitt* production to double McQueen on some of the riskier driving stunts and also to perform one particularly harrowing motorcycle crash scene. Ekins is an inductee into both the Off-Road Motorsports Hall of Fame and the AMA Motorcycle Hall of Fame.

Another occasional McQueen stunt double was Loren Janes, a highly accomplished stuntman and precision driver who first doubled McQueen in his TV series *Wanted: Dead or Alive*, and he also doubled John Wayne on occasion. Among his more whimsical stunt performances was to don a wig and women's swimsuit to double for swimmer Esther Williams for an 80-foot diving shot. One of his most important on-screen stunts came during *Bullitt's* final passages at the San Francisco airport.

Bill Hickman was an inspired choice to play the hitman's partner Phil and the stunt driver in the bad guys' all-black 1968 Dodge Charger R/T 440. Hickman, who was dressed in a black suit and a studious-looking pair of glasses, really looked the part, and he was a more than

well-known entity. By this time, Hickman was already an established Hollywood actor, stunt driver, and stuntman. As an interesting aside—Hickman was friends with the late actor James Dean and occasionally drove Dean's Ford station wagon that towed Dean's famed Porsche 550 Spyder racing car to the track, and Hickman often coached Dean on his driving technique. Hickman was driving the Ford station wagon and empty trailer that followed Dean on the day of his fatal accident in Cholame, California, on September 30, 1955, and was the first person on the scene. He attempted to rescue the grievously injured Dean and assisted his badly injured mechanic, who was also in the Porsche with Dean. Hickman's role in *Bullitt* is a key element of the chase scene's sense of reality, although interestingly enough, he utters not a single line in the film. For a time, Hickman and Bud Ekins were roommates, and Ekins once told me that "Bill was kind of a dingbat, but man could that guy drive!" *Bullitt* was by no means the only prominent movie car chase scene that Hickman helped make famous. He appears in and did a considerable amount of the stunt driving work in

Nearly all of the medical staff you'll see in Bullitt's *famous hospital scenes are working doctors and nurses with this one major exception. This pensive shot shows Don Gordon (left) as Det. Delgetti and Steve McQueen (right) as Lt. Bullitt. The African-American gentleman between them is actor Georg Stanford Brown, who does a solid and credible job as Dr. Willard, who operates on the protected mafia witness after an assassination attempt. Brown, who enjoyed great success as a television and movie actor, learned the medical lingo and looked and moved for all the world like a real doctor during the emergency surgery room scenes. The director wanted Brown to stand in place for a real doctor since he had to deliver lots of lines acting with McQueen and often in conflict with Robert Vaughn's Chalmers, so an actor was called for in these passages. (Photo Courtesy ©/™ Warner Bros. Entertainment Inc. [sl9]; Alamy Stock Photos)*

The French Connection starring Gene Hackman and *The Seven-Ups* with Roy Scheider. Hickman was an ace wheelman to be sure.

Journeyman silver-haired actor Paul Genge portrayed Mike, the shotgun-toting hitman who famously partnered and died with Bill Hickman's wheelman partner Phil. Genge played the heavy murderous mafia thug with aplomb. It was mostly an action part, as he has a single cluster of lines in the film that last no more than 10 seconds. He wore the icy killer look perfectly, wielded a pump shotgun like a pro, and ran and moved well when called for in the script.

Talented and highly acclaimed musician and composer Lalo Schifrin was engaged to develop *Bullitt*'s fast-paced and jazzy musical score, and he delivered on that promise brilliantly. Pre- and post-*Bullitt*, he is best known for his large body of film and TV scores since the 1950s, including the themes from *Mission: Impossible* and *Enter the Dragon*. He has received five Grammy Awards and six Oscar nominations. Associated primarily with the jazz music genre, Schifrin is also noted for his collaborations with Clint Eastwood from the late 1960s to the 1980s, particularly with the *Dirty Harry* films. It is interesting that Schifrin was a somewhat late add to the production, as Quincy Jones was originally on tap to score the film. Jones fell ill and was unable to participate, so Schifrin stepped in at the last minute and proved an inspired, lucky fix for the problem.

Steve McQueen insisted on absolute

realism and that the production make the most of the rich tableau that was San Francisco. Besides its hilly streets, sweeping ocean vistas, and curvy sections that served as the course and backdrop for *Bullitt*'s ultimate movie car chase scene, the script called for scenes in hospitals, nightclubs, an architect's office, and on the runways of an airport. *Bullitt* was filmed at those locations throughout the city.

McQueen generally resented artifice, but since *Bullitt* had his name all over it not only as an actor but also as a product of his production company (with him as star, de facto stunt coordinator, and director), he wanted everything to look, smell, and sound legitimate and authentic. There was no digital green screen or computer-generated imagery in those days, but all too often Hollywood resorted to projecting action sequences onto a screen with the characters or props performing in front of it, all of which was then reshot. More often than not,

this effect yielded a phony look, and McQueen would have none of it and insisted that there would be no sped-up or slow-motion photography allowed.

In an interview regarding the making of *Bullitt*, McQueen famously said, "From the beginning, we felt we should be working in close harmony at a racetrack [to practice high-speed driving together and to help work out some of the stunts]. Bill Hickman, one of the best stunt drivers in the business, and me, one of the worst, went out to Cotati Raceway just outside of San Francisco to work at speeds often well over the tonne mark [100 mph]. It was very hairy sometimes."

When referencing the hospital scenes, McQueen said, "The thing we tried to achieve was not to do a theatrical film but a film about reality. So we did shoot actually in a hospital [San Francisco General], and instead of using actors for doctors, we used doctors. Instead of using actors for nurses, we used nurses."

Steve McQueen as a Racer

McQueen in his black Porsche Speedster leads another similar car. Hollywood sports car–types and SCCA racers loved the lightweight, lithe, open-topped Porsche as a street car you could race, and it was successful for many years in the SCCA's B-Production classes. (Photo Courtesy McQueen Family Collection)

In McQueen's comment where he calls himself out as being "one of the worst" stunt drivers, he was being overly modest in that assessment. Prior to the production of *Bullitt*, he had done more than his share of driving and motorcycle riding for the camera in several of his films. He was also by then an accomplished amateur and professional-level sports car racing driver and motorcycle racer.

Bud Ekins summed it up succinctly: "Steve was just very good physically. He

moved well and was an accomplished martial artist. He could drive a car, race a motorcycle, lag nickels in the alley with a bunch of guys after work, wrangle a horse, shoot a guy, and handle many of his own stunts." He had the physical skills, and of course, he loved hot cars and bikes.

McQueen's racing endeavors began not on four wheels but two. He did a lot of street racing on his earliest Indian motorcycles when he was a young acting student living in

We don't know the context of this humorous happy snap of McQueen hamming up with Porsche/Ford/Shelby driving legend Ken Miles. We believe this location to be the old SCCA Santa Barbara airport racing course in 1959 or 1960, as McQueen was still racing his Porsche at the time and the huge aircraft hangar visible in the background. (Photo Courtesy McQueen Family Collection)

New York. Sometimes he ran just for fun and other times for money. He didn't really begin racing cars until moving to California in 1957. His first new car was a 1958 Porsche 356 Speedster 1600 Super, a nimble, lightweight, street-legal roadster that was more intended for amateur sports car racing. James Dean also raced one for a time. In this little black Porsche, McQueen won his first sanctioned sports car race at the Santa Barbara airfield race course in a Sports Car Club of America (SCCA) productions ranks race in 1959. He enjoyed great success in the Speedster for a while, until (like Dean) he began casting his eye toward a "more serious racing car." The Porsche was sold off in favor of a Lotus 11 Le Mans sports racer.

McQueen spent considerable time in Europe, most particularly England, while he worked on films and did some club-level racing. He befriended (now Sir) Stirling Moss, a famous English all-rounder who had achieved considerable success in Formula 1 (F1), with sports cars, and at Le Mans as a member of the factory Aston Martin team in the late 1950s. This forged the beginnings of a fruitful mentor-mentee relationship between McQueen and Moss, as Stirling recognized that the young American had talent yet needed honing. Moss coached and advised McQueen on the finer details of road racing to the point where he became a fast, consistent, and more-polished racer. His time and experiences in the UK led him to earn a spot on the factory Austin-Healey team for the 12 Hours of Sebring endurance race in Florida in 1962. The Healey cars were production Sprite-based sports cars that were fitted with special aerodynamic roof bodywork to make them faster and more efficient at Sebring. The track featured several long high-speed straights (essentially airport runways) at a former Army Air Corps base. McQueen, who was teamed with British journeyman racer

McQueen and legendary English racer Stirling Moss became fast friends, and the latter coached the former on the finer arts of sports car racing. Moss's connections with the Cooper factory and Austin-Healey teams helped McQueen earn a factory ride at the 12 Hours of Sebring in 1962. He drove well there and the car ran credibly when a mechanical failure caused the car to not finish the race. (Photo Courtesy McQueen Family Collection)

Although he was never world champion, Stirling Moss was a consistently winning Formula 1 driver. It's likely this connection that got McQueen interested in upper-level open-wheel racing. Post-Porsche and -Lotus, McQueen purchased this Cooper Formula Junior car, which ended up being completely destroyed in a fire. (Photo Courtesy McQueen Family Collection)

John Holgate, did not finish due to engine failure and was ultimately classified in 46th place. The die in McQueen's heart was cast in terms of big-game motorsports.

Perhaps due to his friendship with Moss, a driver with many F1 wins to his credit, McQueen elected to sample open-wheel racing. The Lotus was sent packing and traded in for a Cooper Formula Jr., open-wheel racer. He continued racing in a variety of cars and series throughout the mid-1960s to develop his driving skills, which led him back to Sebring in 1970. He teamed with Peter Revson in his own Solar Productions Racing Porsche 908 Series III. The pair delivered a compelling performance (with Steve McQueen's broken foot in a cast, no less) to take second overall, eclipsed only by a flying Mario Andretti in a faster, more powerful Ferrari 512. It is considered by many to be one of the greatest finishes in endurance-racing history and proved without question that McQueen had considerable chops as a racer, which ultimately paved the way for his seminal racing magnum opus film, *Le Mans*, in 1971.

The point here is that in spite of his modesty about the subject, Steve McQueen was a brilliantly capable driver, who was more than up to the job of slinging that Mustang around the streets of San Francisco. This was not only due to his good balance, vision, and all-around physical capability but also the experience he'd gathered by 1968 from at least a decade of motor racing.

McQueen teamed outstandingly with uber-skilled road racer Peter Revson to run this Solar Productions Porsche 908 Spyder at the 12 hours of Sebring in 1970. The pair finished a highly credible, hard-earned second-overall at the famous once-around-the-clock enduro and led the race for a time as several of the factory-entered Ferrari 512s faltered. Had the pair won, it would have been a great "David bests Goliath" story, for sure. (Photo Courtesy McQueen Family Collection)

McQueen and director Yates obviously liked each other, wanted to work together on Bullitt, and did so to great effect and result. Steve McQueen deserves credit for identifying Peter Yates as having the right stuff to direct his action thriller, and equal consideration goes to Yates for understanding that McQueen would want to have creative input on nearly every aspect of the production, most particularly, but not exclusively, his all-important car chase scene. Their creative meetings took place on any given street corner, sitting inside a car, or in this case aboard San Francisco Police Officer Frank Panacci's three-wheeled motorcycle. (Photo Courtesy ©/™ Warner Bros. Entertainment Inc. [sl9])

Director Peter Yates commented about McQueen's commitment to this approach: "Steve digs into characters in such a way as to bring up an original way of portraying an emotion, and he really works like mad to find a way which is right for him and which he can believe in."

McQueen said, "The operation that takes place in the film was done with an actor [as lead surgeon] of course, but with real doctors [surrounding him]. The feelings, the sensitivities that were really in that hospital. This is a kind of reality that's important in motion pictures. If you try to act it, it doesn't come across as if you're really doing it. We had the reality we wanted."

Only two critical casting and costuming decisions remained.

Chapter 2

THE ACTION CAR STARS OF BULLITT

COLOR ME HIGHLAND GREEN METALLIC AND BLACK

Lt. Bullitt's Mustang is more visually modified among the chase-scene pair; it's dechromed and debadged a bit and has louder-than-stock exhaust, a racy set of after-market five-spoke mags and oversize tires. Here you can clearly see the slightly duller paint finish and that the GT emblem on the gas filler cap has been blacked out—all of this perhaps to match more closely with McQueen's (and Frank Bullitt's) independent personality. The Charger remained visually stock right down to the shiny black paint, steel wheels with hubcaps, and whitewall tires. The cars were carefully cast and costumed to match the roles of their drivers, and star McQueen, stunt coordinator Loftin, and director Yates got the looks just right. No wonder they still look good five decades later. (Photo Courtesy © and ™ Warner Bros. Entertainment Inc. [sl9])

Cars have been integral players in film since the silent-movie days. Goodness knows how many Ford Model Ts were destroyed in the often antic-filled films of Laurel and Hardy or the Keystone cops. But seldom in cinematic history (at least up until 1968) have cars been so selectively cast and costumed as they were for *Bullitt. The Solid Gold Cadillac,* a somewhat sappy romantic comedy from 1956, featured a massive Caddy done up to match the film's name, but it wasn't in any other way specially built or customized for the role. The first significant and utterly memorable instance of cars being highly tailored for a film are the famous Aston Martin DB5s specially equipped by MI6's Q Branch for use by James Bond in 1964's *Goldfinger* and the following year's *Thunderball.* Their special defense features included the ability to lay down an oil slick to send any following cars into a spin, onboard machine guns, a rudimentary navigation system, and the famous passenger-side ejection seat. These Astons have often been billed the most famous movie cars of all time.

Lt. Frank Bullitt's rumbling, grumbling 1968 Mustang GT390 fastback and the mafia hitmen's 1968 Dodge Charger R/T 440 Magnum define the same purpose-minded category. They were spec'd out and modified to perform adequately for the chase and hilly jump scenes, and they were equally chosen and costumed for a certain look. As is typical of film production's use, it often takes more than one car to do it all. In this case, there were two Mustangs and Chargers. One of each was designated as the primary stunt performer and the other served more as a beauty or hero car that often remained a bit cleaner and hopefully less damaged than the other that was also used for interior shots of the drivers in the cars, either in motion or for static and still photos.

The good guy's Mustangs were the highest-performing non-Shelby Mustangs offered by Ford at the time. They were equipped with the 390-ci FE big-block V-8 engine that was factory rated at 320 hp. Each was built with a minimum of other equipment to keep the vehicle weight down and maximize performance. The production company acquired two virtually identical and sequentially serial numbered examples directly from Ford. The vehicle identification numbers (VINs) were 8R02S125558 and 8R02S125559.

According to Kevin Marti and his Marti Auto Works company, which has licensed a considerable amount of early Ford production data (including the build sheets and window-sticker data that I've received permission to use), both cars were ordered under special Civic and Government Affairs Vehicle orders in December 1967. They were produced throughout late January 1968 and delivered to the studios shortly after. Decoding the VIN from the data plate shows that both cars were built in Ford's San Jose, California, assembly plant and that they were the two-door fastback bodystyle with the 4-barrel 390-ci V-8 and Ford paint color 3067-A (Highland Green Metallic). They were equipped with Black Vinyl Luxury Buckets Seats, a 4-speed Manual Transmission, a 3.00:1 Conventional Rear Axle Ratio, Extra Cooling Package, GT Equipment Group, F70 14 Wide Oval Nylon Tires, Power Front Disc Brakes, AM radio, Interior Décor Group, Deluxe Seatbelts, Heavy Duty Battery, and single Remote Control Left Hand Mirror. The manufacturer's suggested retail price (MSRP) for each car was $3,802.33 according to the factory window sticker. However, it's likely that the production company bought both cars at wholesale or dealer price (if it paid for them at all) because it's not uncommon for large studios to receive vehicles that play a significant role in a film free of charge in return for the promotional value.

Steve McQueen was known for personalizing and/or mildly customizing his own cars, so it's no surprise that he would also put his fingerprints and personal touch on the vehicles driven by him in character. In this case, the rework involved both the look of the cars and, of equal importance, how they performed.

Enter Max Balchowsky

To amp up the Mustang's already considerable performance and ensure it was up to the punishment it would endure through the driving stunts planned for *Bullitt*, McQueen and the production company turned to Southern California race car builder and racer Max Balchowsky.

McQueen lived in Hollywood and had his own personal stable of interesting sports and racing cars, so he was familiar with Balchowsky's logically enough named Hollywood Motors. Over time, Ina and Max Balchowsky built and campaigned a primarily Buick-powered run of junkyard dog–style sports racers called *Old Yeller* that

DELUXE MARTI REPORT

"CONCOURSE QUALITY, HOBBYIST PRICE"

Marti Auto Works
www.martiauto.com
13238 W Butler Drive
El Mirage, AZ 85335
Phone (623) 935-2558
Fax (623) 935-2579

Ford
Official Licensed Product
5012

Proud to display this symbol

Copyright Kevin Marti 2019

Thank you for your interest in our services. We have determined the following information for your vehicle from the Ford Database we have:
1234567890123456789012345678901234567890123456789012345678 90
8R02S125558   R 6A R 09A2304   KM9A 3654 F2   1 2 D211   7126Z0 B A

DOOR DATA PLATE INFORMATION
Serial Number **8R02S125558**

8	1968
R	Built at San Jose
02	Mustang 2-Door Fastback
S	390-4V V-8 Engine
125558	Serial Number of this Ford scheduled for production at San Jose
63B	Mustang Decor 2-Door Fastback
R	Highland Green Paint, Ford #3067-A
6A	Black Vinyl Luxury Bucket Seats
09A	Scheduled for build January 9, 1968
71	Los Angeles DSO (District Sales Office)
5	3.00 Conventional Rear Axle
5	Four-Speed Manual Transmission

ORDER TYPE: CIVIC & GOV. AFFAIRS VEHICLE
DSO ITEM #: 2304
DEALER #: 71 62Q
LOS ANGELES ASSEMBLY PLANT
BOX 101
PICO-RIVERA CA 90662

Your vehicle was equipped with the following features:
- Extra Cooling Package
- GT Equipment Group
- Optional Axle Ratio
- F70X14 Wide Oval White Sidewall Nylon Tires
- Power Disc Brakes
- AM Radio
- Interior Decor Group
- Deluxe Seat Belts
- Remote Control Left Hand Mirror
- Heavy Duty Battery

This is one of the two Mustangs used for the production of the movie "Bullitt."

Your vehicle was actually produced on January 6, 1968 -- three days ahead of schedule.

Kevin Marti

For Mustang, Thunderbird, Cougar, Falcon, Fairlane, Lincoln, Torino, and other Ford Products

---

NOT FOR TITLE OR REGISTRATION
8R02S125558 WARRANTY NUMBER Ford MADE IN U.S.A.

Ford

63B R   6A   09A 71
BODY COLOR TRIM DATE D.S.O.

IMPORTANT DATES

ORDER RECEIVED:	1
CAR SERIALIZED:	1
BUCKED:	0
SCHEDULED FOR BUILD:	0
ACTUALLY BUILT:	0
RELEASED:	0
SOLD:	0

STATISTICS
Your vehicle was one of:
5,488 With this Paint Code
355 With these Paint/Trim Codes
4,113 With these Engine/Transmiss
3,039 Ordered from this DSO
12,087 With GT Equipment Group
For the 1968 Mustang 2-Door Fastback

DELUXE MARTI RE

"CONCOURSE QUALITY, HOBBYIST PRICE"

Marti Auto Works
www.martiauto.com
13238 W Butler Drive
El Mirage, AZ 85335
Phone (623) 935-2558
Fax (623) 935-2579

Thank you for your interest in our informati
1234567890123456789012345678901234567890
8R02S125559   R 6A R 09A2306   KM9A 3654 F2

DOOR DATA PLATE INFORMATION
Serial Number **8R02S125559**

8	1968
R	Built at San Jose
02	Mustang 2-Door Fastback
S	390-4V V-8 Engine
125559	Serial Number of this Ford scheduled for production at San Jose
63B	Mustang Decor 2-Door Fastback
R	Highland Green Paint, Ford #3067-A
6A	Black Vinyl Luxury Bucket Seats
09A	Scheduled for build January 9, 1968
71	Los Angeles DSO (District Sales Office)
5	3.00 Conventional Rear Axle
5	Four-Speed Manual Transmission

ORDER TYPE: CIVIC & GOV. AFFAIRS VEHICLE
DSO ITEM #: 2306
DEALER #: 71 62Q
LOS ANGELES ASSEMBLY PLANT
BOX 101
PICO-RIVERA CA 90662

Your vehicle was equipped with the following features:
- Extra Cooling Package
- GT Equipment Group
- Optional Axle Ratio
- F70X14 Wide Oval White Sidewall Nylon Tires
- Power Disc Brakes
- AM Radio
- Interior Decor Group
- Deluxe Seat Belts
- Remote Control Left Hand Mirror
- Heavy Duty Battery

This is one of the two Mustangs used for the production of the movie "Bullit

Your vehicle was actually produced on January 8, 1968 -- one day ahead o

Kevin Marti

For Mustang, Thunderbird, Cougar, Falcon, Fairlane, Lincoln,

NO
8

63
BODY

ORDE
CAR S
BUCK
SCHE
ACTU
RELE
SOLD

Your v

4
3
12
For the

These are the window stickers and Marti Report build sheet decoding of the two Mustangs, colloquially referred to by the final three numbers of their VINs: 558 and 559. The former, for no particular reason, was dedicated the stunt car or jumper, while the latter got picked as the beauty or hero example. It's hard to believe how little these cars cost five decades ago. The build sheet analysis gives detailed equipment and options breakdown, plus the timeline of the builds and from which factory they came. This was also back in the day when window sticker prices still included cents instead of just round dollars, as they all do today. (Photos Courtesy Marti Auto Works)

MUSTANG 2PLUS2 FASTBACK
HIGHLAND GREEN
BASE 289 2V 8 CYL ENGINE
390 4V GT 8 CYL ENGINE
EXTRA COOLING PACKAGE
GT EQUIPMENT GROUP
FOUR SPEED MANUAL TRANSMISSION
F70X14 WIDE OVAL WSW TIRES   NC
POWER DISC BRAKES
AM RADIO
INTERIOR DECOR GROUP
DELUXE BELTS
REMOTE CONTROL LEFT H MIRROR
HD BATTERY
302-R-075 WARNER BROS
   WHEN APPLICABLE PRICES INCLUDE 7% FET

MFR'S. SUGGESTED RETAIL PRICE
$ 2712 44
105 63
158 08
12 95
146 71
233 18

64 77
61 40
123 86
15 59
9 58
7 44

BETTER IDEAS
for greater strength, durability, and lasting satisfaction

Ford has a way with better ideas . . . advanced ideas that put you way ahead when you buy, and keep you out front for mile after mile of pure satisfaction!

Better standard equipment ideas like these:

- Ford's unique 2-sided key . . . always right side up
- Suspended accelerator pedal . . . adjusts itself to your foot
- Ford's fully synchronized 3-speed manual transmission . . . lets you downshift to low without gear clash
- Ford's famous Twice-a-Year Maintenance . . . greater economy and convenience

Better optional equipment ideas like these:

- New 302-cu. in. V-8 . . . new power, performance and fuel economy
- SelectShift Cruise-O-Matic . . . fully automatic or smooth-shifting manual, as you choose
- New AM/FM Stereo Radio . . . thrilling new entertainment (not available on Falcon)
- Convenience Group . . . lights remind you to fasten belts, warn if door's ajar, fuel is low or parking brake is on (except Falcon)
- SelectAire Conditioner . . . comfort for all seasons
- Power Front Disc Brakes . . . for smoother stopping power

Ford's better ideas are everywhere in these sparkling '68 models. Better ideas in styling, craftsmanship and quality. Every '68 Ford is equipped with the full complement of Ford Motor Company Lifeguard Design Safety Features.

TRANSPORTATION CHARGES   150 70

TOTAL $ 3802 33

FINANCE NOV 67 AAD 419C (PRINTED IN U.S.A.)

SOLD TO:
LOS ANGELES ASSEMBLY PLANT
BOX 101
PICO-RIVERA   CA 90662
SHIP TO (IF OTHER THAN ABOVE)
MIDWAY FORD SALES
200 N VERMONT AVE
LOS ANGELES   CA

VEHICLE SERIAL NUMBER   FINAL ASSEMBLY POINT
8R025125559   SAN JOSE

METHOD OF TRANSP.

THIS LABEL IS AFFIXED PURSUANT TO FEDERAL AUTOMOBILE INFORMATION DISCLOSURE ACT. MANUFACTURER'S SUGGESTED RETAIL PRICE INCLUDES REIMBURSEMENT FOR FEDERAL EXCISE TAX AND SUGGESTED DEALER PREPARATION AND CONDITIONING CHARGE. GASOLINE, LICENSE AND TITLE FEES, STATE AND LOCAL TAXES AND DEALER INSTALLED OPTIONS AND ACCESSORIES ARE NOT INCLUDED.

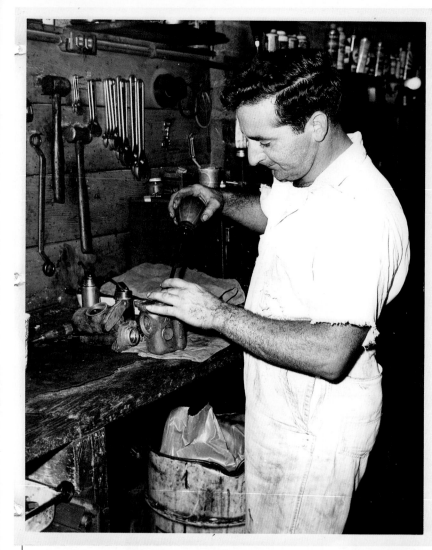

Lithuanian-American, West Virginia-born racer/builder/mechanic Max Balchowsky is at work in his Hollywood shop. His modest yet immaculate garage did a lot of things: maintained a variety of racing cars, including some of the European thoroughbred variety; engine swaps; and of course designing and building his own racers. Equal credit should go to his beautiful and mechanically minded wife, Ina, who herself was a capable welder and fabricator with a solid head for business and ran the paperwork side of the shop. Chassis, frame, and suspension ideas were often drawn out between the two of them using chalk on the shop floor. The Balchowskys used a combination of new, used, and often humble components with hopped-up Buick nailhead V-8 and home-fabricated body panels, combined with modest, clever, and gutsy hard work to beat Ferraris, Maseratis, OSCAs, and other big-name sports car brands. (Photo Courtesy Ernest Nagamatsu Collection)

regularly beat the best from Ferrari and Maserati in the SCCA and other sports car ranks. Carroll Shelby once said that the Balchowskys were America's best back-yard race car builders and racers. It was an inspired choice because the Balchowskys knew how to make cars tough and fast; both elements were needed for this job.

There is conflicting speculation as to how much the cars were modified and what was actually done and addressed. However, according to historian and SoCal vintage racer Ernest Nagamatsu, the Balchowskys applied typical straightforward hot rodding tricks that they learned from their own racing cars to get the Mustangs and the Chargers up to snuff and speed.

"Max had completed (at Hollywood Motors) modifications on the two 1968 Mustang GT390s and the two Dodge Charger 440 Magnum R/Ts," Nagamatsu said. "Max reinforced the shock towers, changed the arc of the leaf springs, added Koni shocks, worked over the Dodge's

CARROLL SHELBY AND MAX BALCHOWSKY
OLD YELLER II, Buick Special, JULY 1960

The one and only Carroll Shelby thought and spoke very highly of the Balchowskys and cited their prowess for clever ideas and an ability to make an often-humble variety of components work to make solid, fast race cars that ran well and with success. Even though Shelby ultimately employed Ford V-8 engines in the creation of his Shelby Cobras, he recognized Balchowsky's brilliance is using the smaller-valved, torquey Buick V-8 in his Old Yeller *sports racers. (Photo Courtesy Ernest Nagamatsu Collection)*

It's likely that this is the stunt/jumper car (chassis 558), given that it's dirty and wearing more than its share of non-hero/beauty-car (chassis 559) scrapes, bangs, and dents, plus a driver's side rearview mirror. This gives a good look at the beefy, wider than factory rolling stock run on the Mustangs. This shot was snapped just prior to the formation of the beginning of the chase scene. (Photo Courtesy © and ™ Warner Bros. Entertainment Inc. [sl9])

the cops there, and they would never stop him."

Several sources have added that Balchowsky performance tuned the factory Ford/Autolite 4-barrel carburetors. A final important modification was to open the Mustang's exhaust systems a bit in the name of more engine sound and increased performance. The stock GT390 exhaust is a true dual system that runs small resonator glasspacks between the transmission and the differential. The little muffs sit just below the floorboards about where the front seats are mounted. A large, dual-muffler unit was mounted transversely aft of the rear axle and finished by chrome twin exhaust finishers that came out each side of the lower rear fascia. Balchowsky elected to leave the mid-mounted glasspacks alone but removed the rear-mounted transverse muffler entirely and replaced it with straight dual-exhaust pipes. The

torsion bars, strengthened steering arms, milled heads, [and] added sway [anti-roll] bars with parts and structural welds being magnafluxed to cover liability concerns. They tested the cars running up in [Los Angeles'] Griffith Park as Max knew all of

Here McQueen is the picture of handsome, focused concentration and is wearing the same sport coat and turtleneck sweater he's seen in throughout the chase. You can see some interesting movie car details, such as the clear windshield with no gradated blue-tint band running across the top section of the glass. This is also a nice look at the Shelby Mustang steering wheel and its Tony Nancy handstitched leather cover. An original of this wheel today is very expensive; although for those wishing to authentically clone their own Bullitt Mustang, an original-looking reproduction piece is now available in the aftermarket. (Photo Courtesy ©/™ Warner Bros. Entertainment Inc. [sl9])

rear exhaust tips were also binned and replaced with unadorned, vertically cut exhaust pipes that exited straight out the back. Mission accomplished. The Mustangs sounded marvelous and likely picked up a few horsepower in the process. The Balchowskys ensured that the cars were tougher, faster, and cornered better than they did when delivered in stock form.

Equally important was the cars' costuming. For the Mustangs, the production company relied on McQueen's painter and body man of choice, Lee Brown. Brown had (and still owns and operates) a paint and body shop in nearby San Fernando Valley and previously customized and/or painted several of McQueen's cars, including his 1967 Mini Cooper S and a rare Ferrari NART Spyder. Brown vividly recalled working in the shop with Steve to divine the right look for Bullitt's Mustang.

"Steve wanted to tone them down a bit, but changing the color was never a part of the plan," Brown said. "[Steve] loved and likely chose the dark green metallic, so that stayed, but he wanted to dull it down and make the car look a bit 'saltier,' which we accomplished with cleanser. I'll never forget taking cleanser and scuffing up the paint on these two gorgeous, brand-new Mustangs. We also removed all the Ford and Mustang badging and painted some of the lower and rear trim in black. We pulled out the Mustang horse and corral and grille-mounted driving lights, leaving a flat-black mesh grille with no ornamentation at all in it. We changed the driver's side mirror to something a little smaller [that] wouldn't be so much in the way of any camera shots taken from the front fender area back in through the driver's window."

The final and perhaps most iconic of visual finishing touches was swapping the stock-style steel wheels for American Racing Torq Thrust D five-spoke mags and much beefier blackwall tires. Both cars were identically modified because they were the same car on camera and had to look as if only a single car was being used and driven by Lt. Bullitt.

Safety steering wheels with padded central bosses were just phasing into production automobiles in 1968, and the Mustang wore one that wasn't particularly racy or attractive. For Frank Bullitt's cars, McQueen binned the new safety wheel and swapped it for a wood-rimmed, polished-aluminum spoked 1967/1968 Shelby GT500 steering wheel. He had his friend Tony Nancy, a drag racer and upholstery shop owner, stitch a neat leather wheel wrap for each one, which offered more grip than the polished mahogany rim of the Shelby piece. The interiors were otherwise left stock. See Appendix A for even greater detail on the upgrades and modifications that the Mustangs received prior to their all-important curtain call.

The story of the bad guys' sinewy black Dodge Chargers is somewhat murkier. Two cars were purchased new from a San Fernando Valley Dodge dealer, and even though both are R/T 440 Magnum models, they were not originally built to exact identical form. A teenaged Anthony

Bologna, who lived near where some of the filming was taking place, was a very lucky, muscle car–headed kid at the time and stumbled onto one of the Chargers while it was awaiting a filming call to action. He asked the car's tender if he could sit inside and if he could see the engine. Once inside, he was somewhat disappointed to see that the car had an automatic transmission because at the time the coolest of American muscle cars had 4-speed transmissions. Once under the hood, he saw what appeared to be a stock and proper 375-hp 440-ci Commando Magnum engine, which was an optional engine choice at the time. In 1968, the Charger could have been ordered with the somewhat-plebian 318-ci V-8 on up to and

When visualizing the cars jumping and bouncing their way down Taylor Street, most enthusiasts think of the Mustang's many hard landings, yet the Charger was no less a high flyer. Note the VW Beetle just off the car's passenger door. It was driven by a crew member and shows up in several edited and repeated passages of the chase scene. Both of the Charger's driver's side hubcaps are still attached in this great action shot. (Photo Courtesy ©/™ Warner Bros. Entertainment Inc. [sl9])

In this day and age of digital GoPro cameras, most no larger than a cigarette packet, this photo demonstrates the amount of hardware, both cameras and microphones plus at least one operator, that it took to rig up the Mustang to capture all the action. If you ever wonder why the Charger appears faster than the Mustang in some passages, it's due to the Dodge's horsepower advantage and the fact that all of this gear (and people) added an easy 500 pounds to the Mustang's overall weight. (Photo Courtesy ©/™ Warner Bros. Entertainment Inc. [sl9])

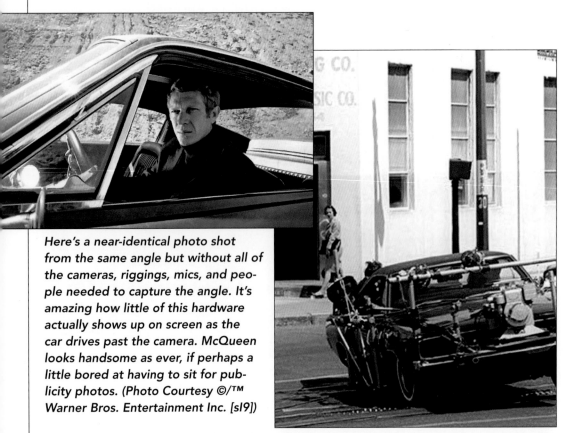

Here's a near-identical photo shot from the same angle but without all of the cameras, riggings, mics, and people needed to capture the angle. It's amazing how little of this hardware actually shows up on screen as the car drives past the camera. McQueen looks handsome as ever, if perhaps a little bored at having to sit for publicity photos. (Photo Courtesy ©/™ Warner Bros. Entertainment Inc. [sl9])

One hardworking Charger: the Dodges, like the Mustangs, also captured a considerable amount of film and sound. Here the Charger wears a bit of an exoskeletal rig to accommodate its several cameras and microphones. Hickman continued as the Dodge's primary wheelman even when rigged up like this. The device mounted right in front of the grille is a generator since much of the equipment on this particular rigging was powered by 110-volt household electricity. In some cases, the smaller equipment was battery powered. (Photo Courtesy ©/™ Warner Bros. Entertainment Inc. [sl9])

After the famous "missed turn and reverse wheel-hopping burnout," McQueen lays down one of the chase scene's most amazing burnouts. Even though the way it happened was a bit of an accident, it all looked so good and so real that McQueen, Yates, and the editors all felt it was best left in the final cut. Who could disagree? (Photo Courtesy ©/™ Warner Bros. Entertainment Inc. [sl9])

including the 440 and top-of-the-line 426 Hemi. It was also a bit confusing that this Charger was painted black with evidence of metallic blue paint on some of the under-hood panels. It is clear from watching Bill Hickman shifting gears during the chase scene that the other Charger was quite possibly factory delivered in black paint and had a 4-speed transmission. Unlike the Mustangs that we know are DNA-matched twins, the Chargers were built somewhat differently: one being blue and the other black, and the former with a 3-speed TorqueFlite floor-shifted automatic transmission and the latter with a 4-speed.

Another interesting equipment choice was that the Charger ran whitewall tires on black steel wheels with hubcaps. This accommodated the stunt team's desire to have the Charger bang into things during the chase scene and send a few hubcaps flying (which is clearly visible in the film), or, more likely, this is the way the cars were built and factory-equipped, and the production company didn't see the need to change the rolling stock. The Charger also ran an optional black vinyl top.

The Chargers were beefed up by the Balchowskys because both cars were subjected to the same high-flying torture on the San Francisco streets. There's no documentation of any engine or performance modifications needed or performed on the Dodges, quite likely because the Charger's 440 had about 50 hp on the Mustang's 390, although Ernie Nagamatsu's notes from the Balchowskys indicate that the torsion-bar springs were modified and beefed up to withstand the punishment of the jump sequences. Several instances existed where the Charger was put into service as a camera car for some of the Mustang's action sequences, which also added weight and incited the need for heavier-duty underpinnings. The narrow whitewall tires didn't offer much traction but made those block-long tire-smoking burnout sequences that much easier.

All the Chargers and Mustangs were wired, rigged, and bracketed for the ability to record sound—not only from the engines but also for all of the squealing, suspension crashing, and fender banging going on between. Plus, they each had welded-on box metal channels that were installed on the car in several locations to handle a variety of camera mounts. Some of them were manned with an operator, and others were either set to run automatically or via driver actuation. When the

Charger was pressed into camera car duty, its trunk lid was often removed so that a camera could be mounted in the trunk area. There was just enough room for a cameraman to sit behind the camera near the back window. One can only imagine that was a particularly risky assignment for a camera operator who drew the short straw that day. It would have been a thrill ride for sure with the camera and the cameraman both sitting high enough to be impacted by the slipstream of the wind as the cars reached and exceeded 100 mph.

Rumor and urban legend often disagree on the number and specification of chase-scene cars used in the production of *Bullitt*. The book *Steve McQueen: The Unofficial Biography* states that four Mustangs were employed to accomplish the chase scene and the balance of filming. Another long-standing rumor is that only two were needed to accomplish the action but that a third identically painted and trimmed car (powered by a stock Ford small-block 302-ci V-8 and backed by an automatic transmission) was used for some beauty shots and ultimately went into service in Warner Brothers Studio's motor pool. I've checked with every known credible source and *Bullitt* guru I can identify, and

none of them agree that more than two Mustangs and two Chargers were needed and employed. No credible source has produced a car, VIN, paperwork, or photographs, beyond hearsay, to substantiate that more than this quartet of chase cars were used to make *Bullitt*. Should that occur, I'll gladly revisit the discussion.

One other critically important member of *Bullitt*'s automotive cast was necessary to capture the high-speed, often side-by-side action between the Mustang and the Charger. A specially designed and built camera car was needed that could not only handle the weight of cameras and camera operators but also do so safely and quickly enough to keep up with the main characters of the chase. Throughout film history, a variety of cars and other vehicles were built or modified for this activity. Notably, Howard Hughes had a 1936 Lincoln Model K V-12 limousine converted for camera car duty. After that unusual machine, Hughes owned a pair of 1950 Chryslers with significantly customized rear bodywork to create a rear deck platform upon which cameras and camera operators could stand. These cars were designed, engineered, and built by the Chrysler factory, and one of them is cur-

Setting up a camera car for Bullitt was by no means the Balchowskys' first rodeo. They knew how to capture fast action sequences from a rolling car. This example is one of their Buick-powered Old Yeller sports racers rigged for a driver (Balchowsky) and an operator for the two cameras. This home-built mongrel racer was used to capture the action in the original The Love Bug from 1968. (Photo Courtesy Ernest Nagamatsu Collection)

rently in the Petersen Automotive Museum's permanent collection. In more recent times, director Hal Needham developed a vehicle called *The Shotmaker*, which is based on a heavy-duty Ford Econoline cab and chassis truck and allowed cameras to photograph cars from a variety of angles at speed. In between all of that, there weren't many vehicles up to the demands of *Bullitt*'s production plans.

The production team already included race car builder and driver Max Balchowsky, so the camera car job was turned over to him. His solution was unusual, innovative for the time, and absolutely effective. It began with a Chevrolet Corvette chassis, which was quite possibly a former racing car, fully stripped of its factory body and cabin. Balchowsky added lightweight, removable roadster-style bodywork to encapsulate the fuel tank and provide support for camera mounts. The small-block Chevy remained up front and ran single carburation. It didn't need to be beautiful (although it appears to have been nicely finished); it just had to be fast.

Given the power-to-weight ratio of a lightweight chassis with very little bodywork, you can bet it was. This car was nicknamed *The Chevy* and usually had at least two cameras with one camera operator in addition to the driver aboard.

As the chase scene progresses out of downtown San Francisco proper, the roads were less hilly but very fast. Bud Ekins famously commented, "The level runs were as wild as the hill stuff. Here was [Director of Photography] Bill Fraker hangin' out of that stripped-down Chevy, sitting on a chair with his camera stuck out there at over 100 mph right down the city street about 6 feet away from me [in the Mustang], while I drove flat-out with the cement poles and light standards whippin' past us."

The cast, crew, and four-wheeled crew members were set. It took nearly three weeks and considerable manpower and planning to accomplish shooting the famous chase.

Yates and McQueen huddle around the Corvette chassis-based camera car that the Balchowskys and Pat Hustis built for use on Bullitt. *This confab certainly took place during the filming of the chase, with McQueen in Lt. Bullitt chase-scene costume. Note that the camera car's light metallic blue body panels appear to be very nicely finished. The Balchowskys' cars weren't fancy or exotic but always well-conceived and built. (Photo Courtesy ©/™ Warner Bros. Entertainment Inc. [sl9])*

Chapter 3

ACTION!
HOW *BULLITT'S* STUNTS WERE PLANNED AND FILMED

Production photography of *Bullitt* began in San Francisco on February 12, 1968, and the chase scene itself was primarily shot during the third and fourth weeks of the production schedule. Each day's filming required about 50 cast and crew members: walkie-talkie-equipped lookouts, the production crew and police to set up and maintain road closures, and staff to drive other vehicles passing through the chase action.

Each of the chase scenes were carefully choreographed by Director Peter Yates, Stunt Coordinator Carey Loftin, Director of Photography Bill Fraker, camera car builder and often driver Max Balchowsky, McQueen, and often stunt drivers Ekins and Hickman. The team usually huddled on the sidewalk at the primary intersection of each scene with a chalkboard in hand, drawing out the scene and the distance between cars. Sometimes the chalk draw-ings ended up on the street or sidewalk surface itself. The chase passages weren't filmed in the order they are seen on the screen. More often, the scenes were driven by where the cast, crew, and equipment were at the moment or the proximity

to a certain street or backdrop. Yates, Fraker, and McQueen wanted to make the very most of San Francisco's identifiable architecture, landscape, and topography. Initially, there was a notion to film part of the chase on the Golden Gate Bridge, but this was vetoed due to the challenges of closing down the bridge for a day or days on end—not to mention the safety risks of a car or crewmember going over the side into the water. Still, the iconic bridge is visible in several of the film's scenes, as is Alcatraz Island and several iconic streets and buildings.

A wide variety of full-sized lightweight cameras, camera locations, and on- or in-car camera mounting rigs were used to capture the action. Often, the Mustang and the Charger themselves served multiple roles, not only being the stars of the chase scene but also being charged with capturing the footage. All sorts of steel tubing were welded onto or into the cars where camera mounts could be inserted. The cars also recorded their own sound to capture all the crashing, banging, redline gear shifts, and tire-smoking burnouts. The aforemen-tioned Corvette chassis–based camera car

Facing Page: This is among the most amazing and detailed photos in this book. There's lots going on here atop the Russian Hill area. Besides all the background scenery, build-ings, and such, this is such a rare shot in that it contains two Bullitts. Not two Bullitt Mus-tangs, but two Frank Bullitts! There's one Lt. Bullitt, cigarette in hand, facing to the right of the photo—that's Bud Ekins in the proper Bullitt jacket, blue turtleneck, and white or tan pants. Look further to the right of the shot and you'll see another Lt. Bullitt in darker pants standing at the doorway of the Mustang—that's McQueen. Fortunately, the two men were close enough physically in terms of hair and eye coloring that when seen inside a flying Mustang, they could easily double. Look at the top of the shot and you'll see the ocean and the harbor, replete with at least one boat visible in shot. All truly a magic moment in time. (Photo Courtesy McQueen Family Collection)

This great production still shot clearly shows most of the Mustang's exterior camera mounts. Look just below the rocker panel line of the car and you'll see the three square-box tubes welded to the chassis that could hold camera and/or sound equipment. Plus, there was a temporary, detachable mount rigged up for the nose of the car, seen here in action with a camera mounted and rolling. In as much as the camera is pointed directly at the driver, there's no question this was McQueen at the wheel. Even though he and double Bud Ekins were of similar stature and features, Steve's jawline and haircut are often easily identifiable as being the Real McQueen. (Photo Courtesy ©/™ Warner Bros. Entertainment Inc. [sl9]; Alamy Stock Photos)

often carried at least two cameras running in front of, behind, or beside the two star cars. In some instances, a camera was placed on a tripod, switched on, and left in static position to wait for the cars to come careening by them. And, of course, camera operators were stationed at strategic locations to capture the action in motion as the cars blazed by. Lots and lots of film footage, and many moving pieces (crew and equipment) were required to capture these once-in-a-lifetime scenes.

An interesting location that is only seen on screen for a moment or two is the 450 Sutter Street garage, although it is depicted as part of Chicago in the opening scenes. This old-school underground parking garage location wasn't only used for these few frames but it also served as a pop-up garage and repair shop for the

Mustangs and Chargers that sustained almost daily damage while filming the chase scene. After the cars *acted* in the filming of the downhill jumping chase scenes, it was inevitable that at least one had oil-pan damage, bent or broken suspension components, and/or a cracked exhaust system. Balchowsky used this garage as a temporary home base to repair them. He didn't have the parts or equipment on set to completely overhaul an engine or transmission, but he had some spare parts and enough welders and tools to keep the cars moving. No one kept records of how many oil pans were bent, damaged, cracked, and then welded on the hard-working stunt cars. It wasn't at all unusual for one of the cars to have no oil left in its crankcase at the end of a particular day or scene. Being a racing driver,

The 450 Sutter Street Garage is as it looked in the fall of 2019, conveniently with a 2019 Mustang Bullitt parked in front, fortunately with no oil pan or other damage reported. There's much more about these fabulous cars in chapter 6.

builder, and mechanic, Balchowsky knew how to get this sort of triage work done quickly and effectively. A car would often show up to the garage smoking, clanging, and rattling after a particularly hard day of shooting, and Balchowsky and one of his mechanics would work through the night to put Humpty back together again and get the car ready for the next morning's call time.

This is a recent look of the 450 Sutter Street garage at just below ground level. During the film's opening sequence (set in Chicago), you'll see a dark-colored Bizzarrini 5300 Strada parked in the bay on the right side of this shot. This is also the building where Max Balchowsky set up a pop-up shop to take care of the cars during production. Balchowsky and the production team had a mobile triage equipment truck that was on set wherever the cars were. It likely contained a modicum of spare parts, tools, and a welder for emergency repairs. At least one time when Ekins was bouncing one of the Mustangs down Taylor Street, he landed hard on the oil pan and ostensibly exploded it. This is where Balchowsky's racing experience paid off, as he did exactly what he would have at the race track if the same malady occurred. The crew jacked up the car, drained any remaining oil from the pan, lit the torch, and welded the pan. Fire danger? No time for that! Once the sump was refilled, action continued.

Director of photography William "Bill" Fraker is on the ground, camera in hand. The location is the intersection of Powell and O'Farrell Streets. The cable car tracks run up Powell Street. The low shot angle is of the Charger pulling up to park and watch the cab and Lt. Bullitt at the phone booth. Note all the people, period signage, cars, and equipment trucks in the background. Of course, lots of the cinematography was captured using full-sized-roll film cameras on tripods as well as all of the cameras mounted on and in cars. A surprising amount of the footage was also done handheld; sometimes in the name of quick action reality, and other times simply in the name of expediency. (Photo Courtesy ©/™ Warner Bros. Entertainment Inc. [sl9])

The Pizza Brothers

The San Francisco Police Department was charged with supporting the production with security, crowd control, and traffic control. Larger scenes often required the use of several officers at any given locale, but there were two officers who were primarily detailed out to the production team's needs: Frank Panacci and Anthony Piazza Sr. Both men were San Francisco natives of properly local Italian descent, and they earned the nickname *The Pizza Brothers*. Whenever the production team called in to request the need for crowd or traffic control, they never asked for Panacci and Piazza, they'd just say, "Send us the Pizza Brothers."

Frank A. Panacci, the late Officer Panacci's son, recalled his father working many long days and earning lots of overtime pay during the production of *Bullitt*. He particularly remembered how friendly, engaging, and appreciative Steve McQueen was to his father and to any of the police officers and detectives who supported the production. Even though the production employed a considerable roster of extras to appear in scenes that would naturally be inhabited by the public, the officers needed to make sure that passersby didn't accidentally wander into too many scenes (which of course still happened) or interfere with the chase scene during a risky stunt passage. Panacci also recalled McQueen personally autographing photos of himself for his father and sisters. All of the action coordination among the crew and the police took place via walkie-talkies. These were not the small, compact, digital handhelds that are common today; they were large, heavy, battery-powered units with long, expandable chrome antennas. Every once in a while, you'll see the end of an antenna creep into the corner of a scene.

Even though Tony and Frank weren't the only officers deployed for the production of *Bullitt*, there's no question that they were the pair who always seemed to be working right in the heart of the action—up close and

McQueen chats up with the locally famous SFPD Pizza Brothers traffic safety and security team. From left, Officers Ray Crosat, center Frank Panacci, and far right Tony Piazza. (Photo Courtesy Frank A. Panacci Collection)

You'll recognize this image of Steve McQueen as Lt. Frank Bullitt from the official movie poster, and it was also used as an 8x10 glossy publicity still. McQueen autographed and personalized one of these photos for each of Officer Frank Panacci's daughters. (Photo Courtesy Frank A. Panacci Collection)

personal with the stars. They never specifically brought or delivered pizza to the set, yet they will always be known and remembered as the Pizza Brothers. Frank's son also remembered homesick cast or crewmembers occasionally stopping by for a home-cooked Italian dinner at his parents' invite.

Not long after production wrapped, Officer Panacci received at the station a letter on

Not to be outdone by his daughters each receiving a personalized autographed photo from the Bullitt star, Steve McQueen also dedicated this great shot of himself and Jacqueline Bisset to Pizza Brother, friend, and fan Officer Frank Panacci. (Photo Courtesy Frank A. Panacci Collection)

Solar Productions stationary. It read
"Dear Frank,
It would be impossible for me to thank you enough for the great contribution you have made to the whole [production] company during our stay in San Francisco.
Warmest Regards, Steve."

This remarkable series of snapshots were taken by an unknown passerby, who is believed to be deceased. Given the quality (or lack thereof) of these images, it's certain these photos were taken in passing by this person on a rather-humble camera. Given the times, it was likely an old Brownie or Instamatic-style point and shoot camera without much technical capability to modulate focus or exposure.

These prints were at some point given to a production crewmember and ultimately made their way into the caring hands of *Bullitt* guru Glen Kalmack. In spite of considerable due diligence, Kalmack was never able to ascertain with certainty the name of the photographer or his or her current status. These snapshots show a wonderful behind the scenes look at the car-wash scene just before the chase scene begins. This shows how many people and how much equipment it takes to set up a given location

The super torquey Chargers could burn-out step for step with the Mustangs. This photo was likely taken after this Charger had some contact with a camera or another automobile, as you'll notice at the very leading edge of the passenger-side front fender is wrinkled but not badly enough to inhibit the travel or steering of the right front wheel. (Photo Courtesy ©/™ Warner Bros. Entertainment Inc. [sl9])

This behind-the-scenes shot during setup shows more equipment trucks and equipment. The Cortez motorhome in the middle of the shot is likely for McQueen's and Duvall's costume and makeup work. You can see the tail of McQueen's Triumph motorcycle at the right side of this photo. (Photo Courtesy Glen Kalmack Collection)

You can clearly see McQueen and Duvall talking prior to the take in the center of this shot. By this point, it appears that the lights, reflectors, and mics are set up and ready for the scene. (Photo Courtesy Glen Kalmack Collection)

The Sunshine Cab Company Ford taxi is in place and the shot is in process. Duvall is visible at the wheel, and McQueen is approaching the car from the rear of the passenger's side. (Photo Courtesy Glen Kalmack Collection)

for a major film shoot. In several of these photos, Steve McQueen is interacting with Robert Duvall in various stages of the scene. The Army Circle Car Wash, which is no longer standing, was located at the corner of Bayshore Boulevard and Marin Street near the Army Street (now Cesar Chavez) exit of Highway 101.

McQueen has now reached the passenger door and leaned in to ask Duvall something. *(Photo Courtesy Glen Kalmack Collection)*

The Mustang is in the parking lot across the street from the car wash. Crew members are still milling about, which means that the shots at the car wash are nearly over and it's time to roll on to the next location or shot. (Photo Courtesy Glen Kalmack Collection)

It's evident the set hasn't yet been broken down due to the lighting reflector on a high mounting stand between the front of the Mustang and the truck behind. (Photo Courtesy Glen Kalmack Collection)

Note the large equipment truck to the right of this shot. You can see the array of lighting and sound equipment and wiring scattered about the property in order to pull off the car wash scenes. (Photo Courtesy Glen Kalmack Collection)

This interesting behind the scenes shot took place fairly early in the sequence of the film, prior to the chase scene. McQueen is wearing the Bullitt costume that he wore for the meeting with Chalmers at a fundraiser tea party at Chalmers' fabulous hilltop mansion to establish that Lt. Bullitt was assigned to protect Chalmers' soon-to-be-deposed mafia witness. This shot was nabbed with McQueen and the production crew as they arrived or departed the house. The Jaguar at left doesn't figure in the film or the chase, and the Ford at left is the car that Bullitt rode in to and from the meeting with Chalmers. The helmeted police officer in the middle of the shot is Pizza Brother Frank Panacci. (Photo Courtesy ©/™ Warner Bros. Entertainment Inc. [sl9]; Alamy Stock Photos)

The chase scene begins with Bullitt's Mustang and the mafia hitmen's Charger making eye contact and not long after the decoy witness is murdered. The chase begins as the Mustang and Charger travel down Columbus Street and stunt driver Hickman reaches down and buckles his seat belt and bangs a hard tire-smoking left up Chestnut Street to ignite the motorized mayhem. Opinions vary as to when the chase really begins because the cars and drivers were obviously sizing each other up prior to the first burnout.

There has been incorrect speculation about the amount of stunt driving McQueen himself performed. For decades, Loren Janes claimed credit for driving most of the scenes. "Not true," said Bud Ekins in a one-on-one interview with me prior

to his passing in October 2007. "Whenever you can clearly see Steve's face, it was him driving. In some of the scenes where you only see the back of Bullitt's head, it's probably me."

Another easy tell is that even though Steve was right-handed, he often wore his watch on his right wrist. Chad McQueen confirmed that his father learned this trick on the streets of New York, so that if he got into a street fight, his opponent wouldn't know if Steve was right- or left-handed.

"I remember after Steve missed that one turn and then did the famous reverse-gear tire-hopping burnout, Loftin or Yates yelled to me, 'Okay Ekins, get in the clothes. You're driving.'"

"They particularly didn't want Steve

Among the many things that makes this wonderful production still photo so compelling is that it shows both cars in one frame. The Charger is in full tail-out mode here, and it's a lucky wonder, due to Hickman's considerable car control, that the big black Dodge's driver-side rear fender didn't collect the 1966 Mustang it appears headed for. Bullitt demonstrated driving talent in spades and to spare. (Photo Courtesy ©/™ Warner Bros. Entertainment Inc. [sl9])

This magnificent shot from inside the Mustang with McQueen at the wheel shows the Charger in front as the pair ambles down Columbus Street with Bimbo's 365 nightclub visible through the Mustang's windshield. Within a heartbeat of this shot, Hickman in the Charger reaches down, fastens his seat belt, and punches the gas while he pulls a hard left turn with its attendant tire melting a smoky burnout onto Chestnut street, which is the moment when the high speed and most exciting passages of the chase scene really begin. (Photo Courtesy ©/™ Warner Bros. Entertainment Inc. [sl9])

Young, beautiful, and talented were Broadway and movie star Neile Adams and up-and-comer Steve McQueen seen here in the street in front of Ms. Adams' (soon-to-be Mrs. McQueen) Manhattan apartment in the late 1950s. Neile is easily recognized (at the top of the group of four people to the left side of this photo) sporting her trademark big smile and pixie haircut. Steve is standing near the driver's door of his Austin-Healey 100-4. Unfortunately, not fully visible with whatever she held in her right hand that blocks her entire head and face is tall, flaming-haired model/actress Tina Louise, who you'll remember as Ginger Grant from the Gilligan's Island TV series. (Photo Courtesy McQueen Family Collection)

Broadway singer, dancer, and actress Neile Adams was first and foremost Mrs. Steve McQueen. They dated in New York in 1956 when she was working on Broadway. She recalled, "I'd never ridden on the back of a motorcycle up to that time, but in our early days, Steve only had bikes, so that's how we went everywhere."

Neile and Steve were married later that same year and settled in California to primar-ily further Steve's acting career and to raise a family. They were each other's first spouses, and Neile is the mother of Steve McQueen's only two children: daughter Terry (1959) and son Chad (1960).

Even though Neile wasn't Steve's offi-cial manager or talent agent, she had great influence over the film roles he auditioned for and the characters he portrayed. He trusted her judgment and put considerable stock in her

A fashionably clad Jacqueline Bissett snags a ride to another filming location with her leading man aboard his ever-present Triumph. This great still was snagged at the top of the Russian Hill area of San Francisco. Notice the clear view of the bay in the background. McQueen began wearing Barbour weatherproof jackets a few years prior when he ran the International Six Day Trial motorcycle event in East Germany, and this rugged British jacket remained an elemental part of his look for the rest of his life. (Photo Courtesy ©/™ Warner Bros. Entertainment Inc. [sl9])

opinion. She supported *Bullitt* as a *star vehicle* for Steve, and the film was a good start to their Solar Productions' planned five-picture joint-venture deal with Warner Brothers/Seven Arts films.

"The original *Mute Witness* novel was an interesting starting place for the screenplay that became *Bullitt*. Steve of course wanted to make it more modern and for it to be set in late-1960s California, not 1950s Manhattan," said Neile. "And of course, you know the book never had a car chase scene in it; that was all Steve and Peter [Yates]. The last thing he wanted was to have the whole thing phonied up on studio soundstages and back lots. Plus, he'd just fallen in love with the hills and streets in San Francisco with that fabulous ocean view visible from nearly everywhere.

"Steve saw *Bullitt* as a classic Western, and during the development process and even on set, he constantly reminded everyone, 'Remember, we're making a Western here.'"

All of the elements of a classic Western were there: good guys, bad guys, the sheriff/ police, and the shootout at the O.K. Corral, which was, of course, the epic car-chase scene. The Mustang and the Charger were really the six-guns.

"Peter Yates was terrific," Neile continued. "He knew how to shoot and direct action. Plus, they had the best stunt team you could assemble. Carey Loftin was the best in Hollywood, and Steve, Hickman, and Bud all knew and trusted each other. Plus, some of the other actors were our best friends, like Don Gordon, who Steve often rode motorcycles with, and Robert Vaughn, who had a wicked sense of humor and with whom we were also personal friends. We didn't know Jacqueline Bisset personally up until that time, but she did a great job as Bullitt's girlfriend Kathy. She was perfect for that."

Neile remains pleased (yet not entirely surprised) at how popular *Bullitt* remains around the world. Wherever she travels, she's constantly asked about it.

"The French pronounce it '*Boolitt*,' and it certainly remains one of Steve's most popular films," she said.

Mr. and Mrs. Steve McQueen on the Bullitt set during production in San Francisco. Neile's decidedly modish haircut, sunglasses, and chain-belted dress are all decidedly late 1960s. Steve is also wearing a then-popular string of beads given to him by some local hippies living around the city at the time. You'll also see a handful of bullets poking out of the bandoleer side of his shoulder holster. (Photo Courtesy McQueen Family Collection)

Lt. Bullitt parks the Mustang at a grocery store parking lot across the street from the Army Circle Car Wash and walks over to meet up with the cabbie portrayed by Robert Duvall. They chat about the movements of mafia witness Johnny Ross since the cabbie carted him around town upon his arrival from Chicago. You'll note here that the Mustang is already showing signs of wear on the set with deep scratches and a dent at the front of the driver's side front fender and a slightly bent hood and front fender. (Photo Courtesy ©/™ Warner Bros. Entertainment Inc. [sl9])

Look closely and you'll recognize Bud Ekins in the Mustang. His profile and haircut is ever so slightly different than McQueen's, and this is the part of town where Bud did a majority of the flying Mustang takes down Taylor Street. (Photo Courtesy ©/™ Warner Bros. Entertainment Inc. [sl9])

driving the scenes where the cars come flying and bouncing down Taylor Street, as that was really dangerous stuff," Ekins continued. "The cars were, for all intent and purposes, out of control, and of course there were cars parked all over the place, plus houses, fire hydrants, fences, telephone poles, light standards, and goodness knows whatever else there was to hit. And of course if Steve got hurt, the production

Hard landing! We can't tell for sure, but it's highly likely that Ekins was at the wheel as the Mustang launches and bounces its way down Taylor Street. It looks like Ekins has just landed as the front tires are on the ground and the rears may just be touching but the suspension is still fully drooped from its expansion for that instant the car was airborne with all the car's weight off the springs. You'll notice the ever-present green VW driven by a crew member, which appears in the chase sequence several times (see chapter 4). (Photo Courtesy ©/™ Warner Bros. Entertainment Inc. [sl9])

McQueen, at the wheel of the Mustang, approaches a complex pair of right turns at the intersections of Lombard, Larkin, and Chestnut streets and inadvertently sets up one of the most interesting aspects of the chase scene. (Photo Courtesy ©/™ Warner Bros. Entertainment Inc. [sl9])

Even though the way it happened was a bit of an accident, it all looked so good and so real that McQueen, Yates, and the editors all felt it was best left in the final cut. Who could disagree? The most impressive aspect of the whole stunt is that even after McQueen blows the turn, he calmly grabs reverse, looks behind, burns the tires going backward, corrects his course, hits first gear, and blasts up Chestnut Street to convincingly complete the double right turn move. (Photo Courtesy ©/™ Warner Bros. Entertainment Inc. [sl9])

Another great shot shows the three most famous cars in the Bullitt chase scene: Lt. Bullitt's Mustang, the bad guys' high-flying Charger 440, and the green VW. (Photo Courtesy ©/™ Warner Bros. Entertainment Inc. [sl9])

McQueen often kept a motorcycle as his personal transport around movie sets, as it's easy to just hop on and go to the nearest shot location at a moment's notice. And, of course, a bike can be parked nearly anywhere out of the way in these often restricted parking areas. We don't know the story behind the big Jag sedan parked just behind where Steve and his Triumph are sitting, but the belief is that it belonged to director Yates, whose back we see in the right side of this shot. (Photo Courtesy ©/™ Warner Bros. Entertainment Inc. [sl9])

would be majorly stalled or scrubbed altogether. So just to make sure he didn't get upset about it, which he didn't, what they would do is give me a 6 or 7 a.m. call time to come drive those stunts, and then gave Steve something like a 10 a.m. call time so we'd be all done by the time he showed up. He was never angry with me about it, but he used to kid me about it because he had to go on the TV talk shows and tell everyone that it was actually Bud Ekins [who] rode the famous motorcycle jump scene in *The Great Escape*, and now he'd have to go on *Johnny Carson* again and say that it was the same stunt double (me) [who] drove those crazy downhill-jump scenes in *Bullitt*."

One amazing mistake from the chase scene action occurred at the corner of Larkin and Chestnut streets, where the Charger makes a careening right turn and drifts wide, taking out a stationary camera with its left front fender. In the original print of the film, this is clearly seen and heard, marked by a quick yellow/red flash the instant the car collects the camera. It isn't clear if this is any sort of flame or, more likely, a reflection of the sun. It's a hallmark of the original edit, and sadly the red flash has been edited out of most subsequent DVD versions of *Bullitt*.

Another passage where Steve McQueen, Bud Ekins, and Carey Loftin agreed it would be best for Loftin to drive appears near the end of the chase in the Guadalupe Canyon Road scenes where a motorcyclist lays down his bike in front of the careening Mustang. Ekins, being a superior cyclist and racer, was the guy on the bike (in this case well-protected with metal and leather pads and panels beneath his clothes), and Loftin was at the wheel of the Mustang. After some practice, the scene was captured in a single take with a flawless laydown by Ekins and *controlled* out-of-control driving by Loftin aboard the Mustang.

Given the look of the cars and the hard cornering angles, only the sharpest eye will notice that this photo was taken far post 1968 and that the cars are convincing clones or tributes of the movie cars. This photo was taken at a Bullitt Anniversary celebration in Germany. The big giveaway is that the Charger is running radial tires, which existed in 1968 but were much less prevalent on American cars. Both movie cars ran bias-ply tires. However, there's still great action with great-looking cars. (Photo Courtesy Anthony Bologna Collection)

Here the Mustang and Charger set up the final scene where they roll down a hill while tethered together [although not visible in this shot], still trading paint and trying to end it for the other. (Photo Courtesy ©/™ Warner Bros. Entertainment Inc. [sl9])

The Mustang spins out a couple of times during the Guadalupe Canyon chase sequences. The first time, it spins to avoid a rider (stuntman Bud Ekins) laying down his motorcycle to avoid the two cars. Another time is right at the end of scene as the Charger careens into the gas station. The Mustang passes by then spins in the dirt, its front suspension hanging over a ditch, ostensibly ending the scene and grounding the car. (Photo Courtesy ©/™ Warner Bros. Entertainment Inc. [sl9])

In spite of great stunt work, a clever quick-release mechanism nearly didn't work to separate the tethered Mustang and Charger and detonate lots of explosives as the final and ultimate end to the chase scene. The timing of the release of the driverless Charger from the Mustang, the aim of the vehicles, and the actuation of the explosives were close but slightly imperfect. No matter, a considerable amount of great work in the editing room—and lots of good luck—saved the shot, and Bullitt's all-important car chase, and the mafia hitmen bad guys, were done. (Photo Courtesy ©/™ Warner Bros. Entertainment Inc. [sl9])

Depending on the moment that you identify as the beginning of the chase, it lasts about 10 minutes from the initial engagement and burning rubber to a very definitive and explosive ending. The last high-speed moments of the chase (including the previously noted motorcycle-laydown sequence and lots of fender banging and shotgun firings) take place on what was then Guadalupe Canyon Road, which is technically in Daly City, just south of San Francisco proper. This is a fairly wide-open section of mountain highway that allows for long vistas of the twisty two-lane road as well as seriously high speeds near and often above 100 mph. This area isn't nearly as developed or densely populated as the scenes shot in San Francisco, which created different opportunities and challenges than those presented in the city.

The production team determined that the scene should end (and thus put an end to the Mafia hitmen who murdered the decoy witness) in a fiery explosion at a gas station. It was theoretically at the end of the Guadalupe Canyon Road (now Parkway) passage. This area had little population, and the roads were wide open. Thus, it was the logical choice over doing a crash-and-burn scene in the heart of the city. There was no gas station at the spot deemed most appropriate, so the production construction crew set about building a facade building with dummy gas pumps that looked enough like a real filling station so that a car could slam into it and blow up.

The idea was that the Mustang and Charger would come rolling down a hill at high speed, banging into each other door to door, each trying to send the other flying and spinning. By this time, the action was already wound trigger tight with hitman Mike in his Charger shooting with a shotgun at Lt. Bullitt in his Mustang. The trick was determining how to bring both cars down the hill side by side at the same speed and then send one of them flying into the gas station without real people in it.

The solution was ingenious. The two cars would be tethered together (the Mustang's passenger's side to the Charger's driver's side) at the chassis level (below the doors and rocker panels) via a fabricated metal quick-release mechanism triggered by the driver of the Mustang (Loftin in this case). To ensure a quick and clean release between the two cars, this device employed percussive charges somewhat like shotgun shells to fire the steel tubing apparatus apart between the two cars. The Charger would have no driver and only mannequin occupants aboard, so Loftin's accuracy in aiming the Charger at the gas station was critical, as well as his ability to maintain course as the Mustang spins out and away. Balchowsky then cranked away on the Charger's front-end wheel alignment settings so it would steer straight on its own once released from the Mustang.

It worked—but not perfectly. Loftin's aim at the station wasn't dead on, but ultimately it was close enough. It is recorded that he might have released the Charger a moment early, and for a heartbeat it looked as if the Charger could miss the building. Luckily the faux gas station was packed full of dynamite and a crew member hit the trigger to set off the explosion, also a beat early. But under the famous Hollywood doctrine of "we can save it in post-production," there were enough cameras rolling to capture the action at a variety of angles so that a bit of clever editing saved the day. The Charger ends up exploding in the building, and the two bad guys are done for good. Perhaps it's no surprise that editor Frank P. Keller earned *Bullitt*'s only Oscar win in the category of Best Film Editing.

The chase was filmed in a variety of disparate locations and there is little continuity in that sense. It took two weeks to film the chase, which is not surprising because the locations are spread out over a considerable part of the city. The lack of pure route continuity is due to the logistics of filming in a working city. There are several basic locations from which the film crew operated, and many shots were filmed at locations close to these areas. For example, San Francisco General Hospital is close to the chase scenes filmed around 20th Street, Kansas Street, and Rhode Island Street, while Russian Hill served as the base for many of the chase scenes with the Marina District only a short distance away.

The chase segment begins about 65 minutes into the film with the Charger trailing the Mustang near the intersection of Potrero and Army streets in Bernal Heights. This is about where Bullitt notices the black Charger for the first time. It then proceeds west on Army Street (now Cesar Chavez Boulevard) for a few blocks. Bullitt makes a U-turn on Army at Precita. Note the Pontiac and the lighting; in the very next frame it's magically a 1956 Dodge Coronet and with different lighting. Bullitt then makes an immediate right turn on York Street.

The Charger follows Army eastbound and is visible just before they make the right onto York. He disappears up York Street, and the bad guys stop at the corner of York and Peralta and look west trying to find him. They continue on York.

The two cars then magically appear on 20th Street at Kansas Street in the Potrero Hills District, where McQueen appears in the Charger's rearview mirror, which is an iconic moment within the chase scene. They continue north on Kansas Street for about two blocks.

The chase then suddenly jumps to the Russian Hill/North Beach area. It heads east on Filbert Street with Coit Tower and Saints Peter and Paul Church at the corner of Taylor visible in the center of the frame. The chase crosses Mason Street, where the cable car is shown, and then heads northwest on Columbus Avenue past Greenwich Street and the North Beach Playground (now named after Joe DiMaggio) through North Beach. At Chestnut and Columbus, home of Bimbo's 365 nightclub, the bad guys make an illegal left turn (note the white Pontiac Firebird) and head west

(uphill) on Chestnut. In this view looking east on Chestnut, the San Francisco Art College is visible.

They then make a left on Leavenworth and head south toward Lombard. The chase continues at the intersection of 20th and Rhode Island in the Potrero Hills District. They continue on 20th Street and turn right to head north on Kansas. Once again, the chase makes a gigantic leap back into the Russian Hill District. The Charger appears and makes a right turn onto Larkin Street (heading north) from Lombard (headed west). They continue for one block on Larkin.

At the corner of Larkin and Chestnut streets, Bill Hickman gets the Charger into a serious oversteer and then overcorrects and crashes into a 1956 Ford parked at the corner. The crash itself can be seen in the movie from one camera angle but the shot from the second camera angle was not used in the film. In a seriously impressive demonstration of his driving skill, Hickman is seemingly unaffected after the impact and continues east on Chestnut Street.

McQueen attempts to follow the Charger as it turns right on Chestnut and heads east. The Mustang understeers badly, and he is forced to stop and back up to make the turn. This chattering, wheel-hopping reverse burnout is one of the most iconic images of the entire chase scene, and it's unquestionable that McQueen was driving this scene. This missed turn, reverse burnout, and subsequent burnout up Chestnut was an unintended goof, and the editor's original notion was to crop the entire sequence out of the final cut, but McQueen and Yates thought it looked so cool that the decision was made to leave it in. Talk about a good call.

They then appear heading west on Chestnut and turn south on Jones (you can see the street sign and the distinctive building at Jones). They continue south on Jones Street, make another left from Jones onto Lombard, and head east on Lombard.

The locale now shifts to what is probably the most famous part of the chase. They continue north (downhill) on Taylor, pass Green Street, approach Union Street, pass Union Street, and arrive at Filbert Street. They turn left, head west on Filbert, and pass the Chinatown campus of San Francisco City College. At this point, the film editors inserted footage from different uphill-facing camera angles of the procession down Taylor Street.

During this portion of the chase, a crew member-driven green Volkswagen appears in the path of the Charger and the Mustang several times. It is the same green Volkswagen in each frame. There are also two Pontiac Le Mans cars (one white, one green) that show up in several frames and always appear in front of the chase, which is an obvious lapse in continuity. The reuse of the Taylor Street footage may have gone unnoticed were it not for the green Volkswagen. Another car, a Pontiac Firebird, also appears in several sequences. Once at Bimbo's 365 at Columbus and Chestnut, and again on Larkin Street at Francisco.

The chase then winds up on Larkin Street again, and this time the two cars pass Chestnut Street and continue on Larkin. The Dodge Charger hits the wall where Larkin Street curves left and becomes Francisco Street and loses another hubcap that magically is reattached in later frames. Note the white Pontiac Firebird. The cars head down Francisco past Polk Street. Galileo High School, which still stands, is visible behind the rearview mirror.

They continue north on Laguna, which turns into Marina Boulevard. You can see a gas station above and behind the Charger in this frame. It was located across Laguna Street from the Safeway parking lot but is no longer there. The entire area is a grassy hill within Fort Mason and now part of the Golden Gate Recreation Area.

The chase passes the famous Safeway supermarket, which is still in operation, and Fort Mason. The railroad tracks, which connected Fort Mason's piers with the Presidio of San Francisco, are gone. The chase continues west toward the Golden Gate Bridge on Marina Boulevard. This sequence features several repeats with the cars passing the Fort Mason area and the Safeway twice.

The chase was supposed to continue across the Golden Gate Bridge but the Golden Gate Bridge and highway district refused permission because even in 1968 it would have created a traffic nightmare. So, the chase picks up again on University Street, which is all the way across the city to the south.

The chase continues on Market Street in Daly City and heads eastbound past John F. Kennedy Elementary School at 785 Price St. and Guadalupe Canyon Parkway. It continues eastbound on Guadalupe Canyon Parkway. At various points during the eastbound portion, the San Francisco Bay is clearly visible. The direction changes and the cars are shown heading westbound and pass through the same road cut they passed through headed east. In the scene where stunt driver Bud Ekins lays down a motorcycle, there are several radio towers visible on the hill in the background. Those towers are still there and this section today looks very much like it did in the film. Shortly afterward, the chase ends when the Charger crashes in flames at a gas station at the corner of Guadalupe Canyon Parkway and North Hill Drive in Brisbane, San Mateo County.

Chase scene route information reprinted courtesy Ray J. Smith.

Another great tail-out understeering shot of the Charger seemingly looks like it's headed for the back end of a Mustang. Note how hard the car is cornering on its left front tire, magically still attached to the rim and with its hubcap intact. Among the most charming continuity goofs in the entire chase scene is that the Charger loses several of its hubcaps in various passages, only for them to be magically reattached in later scenes. (Photo Courtesy ©/™ Warner Bros. Entertainment Inc. [sl9])

It wouldn't be San Francisco without the city's famous cable cars as Bullitt stalks the bad guys. The famous Coit Tower is partially visible at the top of this shot. (Photo Courtesy ©/™ Warner Bros. Entertainment Inc. [sl9])

The chase follows a fast run down Marina Boulevard, near the water. This street and many of its surrounding buildings look much the same today, although the skyline in the background has evolved considerably. Note how the Mustang's suspension noticeably loads up during this high-speed, sweeping right-hander. (Photo Courtesy ©/™ Warner Bros. Entertainment Inc. [sl9])

Another great high-speed shot as the chase sweeps down Marina. This appears to be McQueen at the wheel. (Photo Courtesy ©/™ Warner Bros. Entertainment Inc. [sl9])

Near the end of filming the chase scene, the production crew, cast, and cars make their way to the Guadalupe Canyon Road area of Daly City. Once the cameras are rolling on a movie set, things happen quickly. But during transportation breaks and shot setups, time seems to stand still and give everyone a few minutes to cool down, or in this case a smoke break. McQueen appears nonplussed while waiting for things to happen. When the downtime is really extended, cigarettes, books, and magazines may give way to a Frisbee bout. (Photo Courtesy ©/™ Warner Bros. Entertainment Inc. [sl9])

Chapter 4

OTHER GREAT CARS IN BULLITT

Besides the hero Mustang and Charger, there are so many other interesting cars featured in *Bullitt*. Some play important roles and others are just a variety of 1950s and 1960s hardware parked up on the street, driven by others, or seen passing by in various scenes. Some are quite plebian, and others are now highly collectible.

There are too many old trucks and such to count, as well as countless Buicks, Caddys, and Chevys, including mid-1950s Bel Air coupes. Most of the San Francisco PD squad patrol cars and sedans used by the detectives are much as you'd expect from a film produced in 1968. They are primarily 1966/1967 Ford Galaxies. The ambulances in several scenes are also a marked departure from the EMT vans and vehicles that are commonly used by today's fire departments and other emergency medical providers. One used in an early hospital scene features a custom rear ambulance body mounted on a mid-1960s

Anyone watching Bullitt for the first time will invariably mention the green VW that keeps showing up in the chase scene. It's also fair to say that along with the Mustang and the Charger, this humble but now-famous Bug is among the most notable cars featured in the film. (Photo Courtesy ©/™ Warner Bros. Entertainment Inc. [sl9]; Alamy Stock Photos)

This monster, somewhat Christine-like, Plymouth Fury is just one of the many dozens of the now–special interest cars constantly prowling the street scenes of Bullitt. Yet in 1968, most of them were little more than 10- to 12-year-old used cars. Certainly the Mercedes-Benz SL, Aston Martin, and Austin-Healey were interesting at the time, but for the most part, whichever car was parked within a given shot location, or drove by during a shot, earned itself a small place in movie history by being there. (Photo Courtesy Glen Kalmack Collection)

Steve McQueen's personal Jaguar XK-SS was photographed near his home in the Hollywood Hills area of Los Angeles. In the opening scene set in Chicago, the camera passes by a low-slung, dark-colored sports car with curvy front fenders and covered headlights, which in the film is actually a Bizzarrini 5300 Strada and is commonly mistaken for this Jag. The Bizzarrini is Italian and a closed coupe; the Jaguar is British and an opened-topped roadster. The scene is somewhat shadowy, so it is not a difficult mistake or assumption to make, but pay close attention and you'll see the differences between this Jag and the Italian GT.

International truck cab and chassis. Another ambulance is a custom-bodied Cadillac sedan. Prosecutor Walter Chalmers gets around town in a 1968 Lincoln Continental limo. In an odd twist of irony, Mr. Chalmers spends much of the film chastising and alleging the incompetence of the San Francisco Police Department and threatens to have Lt. Bullitt prosecuted and pulled from the police force, yet his Lincoln limo wears a bumper sticker that reminds onlookers to "Support Your Local Police." Don't miss the massive and elegant Rolls-Royce Phantom V limousine parked in front of Mr. Chalmers's house early in the film where Bullitt and Chalmers first meet.

A particularly interesting car in the parking garage scene that was set in Chicago but filmed in San Francisco was a dark green Bizzarrini Strada 5300, which is commonly mistaken for McQueen's own Jaguar XK-SS. It's an easy and somewhat logical mistake to make because McQueen's personal Jag and the Bizzarrini both have rounded front fenders, Plexiglas-covered or glass headlights, and are painted dark green. It wouldn't be illogical for McQueen to have one of his own cars on set in San Francisco, but look closely and the differences are easy to spot. The Jaguar is a two-seat, open-topped roadster, whereas the Bizzarrini is a closed coupe with a fastback roofline.

The Sunshine Cab taxi driven by Robert Duvall that is featured prominently in several scenes prior to the chase is a 1967 Ford Galaxie. Everyone notices the green VW that appears multiple times in the chase scene. This is for several reasons: least of all because it seems to be in the way of the action, and for the fact that it makes multiple appearances in the chase because footage of the VW-rolling-through

This amazing street scene with Lt. Bullitt and the Sunshine Cab cabbie, played by Robert Duvall, shows the interest and spectacle of what the filming of Bullitt *in the heart of San Francisco meant to the locals and why the San Francisco Police Department was called in for crowd control. McQueen was a major international star by this time, and him working in town was big news. Director Yates, in a brown sport coat and beige turtleneck, stands just behind the camera, while the tall man to his left with the gray hair and beard is director of photography and action cinematographer William Fraker. (Photo Courtesy ©/™ Warner Bros. Entertainment Inc. [sl9]; Alamy Stock Photos)*

Beautiful people, beautiful car. By this moment in the film, the chase scene is already done, and Lt. Bullitt's Mustang had been damaged or totaled to the point of being undriveable. When he's called to the scene of a murder related to mafia witness Johnny Ross, girlfriend Cathy (Jacqueline Bisset) needs to taxi Bullitt around, such as to the murder scene at a motel in this case. The car is a charming and decidedly sporty Porsche 356 Cabriolet, which is absolutely appropriate for the lovely, educated architect Cathy. Note that Bullitt is on the phone. Handheld radio telephones were extremely advanced and rare for the day, but it's not unusual that a police detective assigned to a high profile case would have one. (Photo Courtesy ©/™ Warner Bros. Entertainment Inc. [sl9])

scene is used, edited, and reused several times in the final cut.

Early in the film when the taxi takes Johnny Ross to the Mark Hopkins Hotel, its parking lot is swimming in upper-crust hardware, including a silver 1968 Aston Martin DBS coupe and Bentley Continental S3 Flying Spur.

A smorgasbord of other interesting sheet metal passes by regularly. This includes but is not limited to at least one Mercedes-Benz 190SL roadster, several Porsche Speedsters and Cabriolets, a 1958 Fiat 1100 sedan, an Austin-Healey 3000 that appears multiple times, and practically too many Mustangs, Camaros, Firebirds, and Corvairs to count. During one of the many scenes filmed directly in front of Frank Bullitt's apartment, a large black 1937 Packard sedan is parked out front. Of course, neither Bullitt nor his girlfriend Cathy drove an old Packard; that car belonged to Bud Ekins.

A car that would be a delight to own, and certainly worth big money today, was the light-yellow Porsche 356C T-6 Cabriolet that belonged to Bullitt's girlfriend Cathy. It was driven to a crime scene with both McQueen and Bisset aboard. How this car was procured for the production is unknown, as is its VIN, and no one ever made public claim to owning this car or offered proof of its provenance as the car used in the making of *Bullitt*. It may have belonged to a member of the cast or crew—or it may have been rented or borrowed for the production. As of this writing, it remains among *Bullitt*'s mysteries.

Here's another interesting shot of Bullitt on his radio phone. Notice that the handset is an old-fashioned, heavy black plastic-cased piece that would have looked at home in Ozzie and Harriet's kitchen on TV back in the 1950s, and that the battery and transmitter unit were so large and heavy they came in their own backpack. Of course, that was all so 50 years ago. (Photo Courtesy ©/™ Warner Bros. Entertainment Inc. [sl9])

This amazing 35-mm negative proof sheet isn't so much about other cars on set as it is a kaleidoscope of images captured by one of the on-set production still shooters on a single roll of black-and-white film. You'll notice a motorcycle parked on the street at the right edge of frames numbers 2 and 3. It appears to be a match for the Triumph McQueen rode around while up in San Francisco, and it's a good bet this is his own bike, parked out of the way during the shooting of scene. Frames 17 through 23 show McQueen taking a smoke break while sitting aboard the same bike. Both the Charger and Mustang feature in this outstanding singular roll of film. I wonder where it is today. (Photo Courtesy ©/™ Warner Bros. Entertainment Inc. [sl9]; Alamy Stock Photos)

Chapter 5

IT'S A WRAP
MUSTANGS AND CHARGERS
LOST AND FOUND

For a time, no one seemed to know where any of the original Bullitt Mustangs went postproduction. We know the 558 stunt/jumper (pictured) was heavily damaged in the final scene of the big chase and was headed toward the scrap heap. Nobody, other than the Robert Kiernan family, knew where and what happened to 559, the hero/beauty car. Contrary to common speculation, the Kiernans weren't hoarders but were subtle and private in their approach to the holy grail of Mustangs. (Photo Courtesy ©/™ Warner Bros. Entertainment Inc. [sl9])

Location filming of *Bullitt* wrapped on May 25, 1968. The production team packed up the remaining cars and gear, and everyone on the cast and crew headed for home. *Bullitt* was produced on an initial budget of $4 million, although records are not clear as to whether the costs exceeded or met that number. It is certain that the transportation and hotel bill for a major Hollywood film would far exceed that today.

One of the Chargers was destroyed in the explosion during the final moments of the chase scene. The primary stunt Mustang (chassis 558, as identified by the final four numbers in its VIN) sustained substantial suspension damage during the spinout scenes filmed in Guadalupe Canyon. It was declared a total loss and committed to the crusher. The postproduction plan for the remaining Charger isn't known. The Mustang 559, the hero or beauty car, was sold

The fate of the Chargers seemed to be a bit more like that of Amelia Earhart or Jimmy Hoffa. One car was confirmed totaled, in fact exploded, in the final passage of the chase scene, while the other simply evaporated. It's a shame no one credible has come forward with concrete proof of their VINs or the whereabouts of the surviving Dodge. (Photo Courtesy ©/™ Warner Bros. Entertainment Inc. [sl9])

to a Warner Brothers studio employee.

Thus began an odyssey that lasted nearly 50 years: where are the cars from the filming of *Bullitt*?

Likely the most amazing backstory of the current location of a *Bullitt* car is attached to the "jumper" Mustang (chassis 558). Somehow it escaped a date with the

Robbie Kiernan, wife of Robert Kiernan Jr. and mother of Sean Kiernan, often drove the famous Mustang, which was hiding in plain sight, back and forth to work most days. Based on Robbie's bellbottom pants, it's likely this photo was snapped in the mid-1970s. (Photo Courtesy Kiernan Family/Ford Motor Company)

WARNER BROS. INC.

4000 WARNER BLVD. · BURBANK, CALIFORNIA 91505 · (213) 843-5115

CABLE ADDRESS: WARBROS

April 16, 1970

TO WHOM IT MAY CONCERN:

This will certify that the green Ford Mustang which was used in the theatrical motion picture entitled "BULLITT," engine number 8R02S12559, bearing California license plates VVE 590, was purchased from the Ford Motor Company by an employee in our Film Editorial Department, Mr. Robert M. Ross. In the picture "BULLITT," California license plates JJZ 109 were used on the car.

Yours very truly,

WARNER BROS. INC.

By _George Phillips_
GEORGE PHILLIPS
Head, Transportation Department

This amazing letter from Warner Brothers Studios certified that the 559 Mustang was sold out of its motor pool to Robert Ross in April 1970. It led a busy life for several years in the 1970s and was resold multiple times. (Photo Courtesy Ford Motor Company)

SOLAR PRODUCTIONS, INC.

14 December '77

Mr. Robert Kiernan, Jr.
13 Prospect Street
Madison, New Jersey

Dear Mr. Kiernan,

     Again, I would like to appeal to you
to get back my '68 Mustang. I would like very
much to keep it in the family in its original
condition as it was used in the film, rather than
have it restored; which is simply personal with
me.

     I would be happy to try to find you
another Mustang similar to the one you have,
if there is not too much monies involved in it.
Otherwise, we had better forget it.

     With kindest regards, I remain

       Very truly yours

       STEVE McQUEEN

8899 BEVERLY BOULEVARD, SUITE 501, LOS ANGELES, CALIFORNIA 90048 • (213) 278-8600 • CABLE: SOLARPIC

This is proof positive that Steve McQueen really wanted what was believed to be the only remaining Mustang from the making of Bullitt. However, by this time the Kiernans loved their car and simply had no interest in selling or trading it for the replacement that McQueen offered them. It remained in the family, quietly hidden away for decades. Talk about a barn find! (Photo Courtesy Ford Motor Company)

The ideal plate for the 559 car would have of course been "BULLITT," but that wouldn't have worked in the 1970s, as personalized plates were limited to six characters. Robbie Kiernan's method was clever and effective. Even though the middle "L" was dropped, the movie reference was more than clear as worn by this car. (Photo Courtesy Ford Motor Company)

crusher and wound up in Mexico. Along its south-of-the-border trail, it was hastily reassembled, painted a variety of colors (blue and then white), and on the streets of Mexico for some years as a daily driver. Imagine that: one of the most famous movie cars in film history wearing a two-hour backyard paint job, pounding around the streets of Mexico for decades in anonymity.

The chassis number 559 hero or beauty car followed a less mysterious path. However, it ultimately went into long-term hiding. After the film was completed, Warner Brothers sold the car to a studio employee named Robert Ross reputedly for about $3,500. Ross kept and owned the car for two years and sold it in 1970 to New Jersey Police Detective Frank Marranca— now the second detective named Frank to own the car. Marranca kept the car in Jersey for about four years, advertised it for sale in *Road & Track* magazine, and sold it in 1974 to Robert and Robbie Kiernan. The Kiernans treated the car much like an everyday driver. Robbie was a school teacher and drove the car to and from work most days.

On December 14, 1977, Steve McQueen wrote a letter to the Kiernans to ask them if he could purchase the car.

McQueen made it a point to note that he wanted the car to be kept original and unrestored, as it was used in the production of the film. It's interesting insight into his knowledge as an enthusiast/collector because the automotive preservation movement had not crystalized in the 1970s. No one valued patina yet; everyone wanted his or her car in shiny pristine condition. The notion of preserving the car's numerous scrapes and bangs hadn't yet matured into the outlook that so many historians and collectors value today.

Although the letter begins somewhat earnestly, it ends with a tone that the Kiernans felt to be somewhat dismissive, so they didn't respond to the letter. Robbie Kiernan purchased the personalized New Jersey state license plate reading "Bulitt" for her husband as a birthday present in 1979. Note the slightly modified spelling used on this plate. At that time, personalized license plates in New Jersey and most other states were limited to six letters, numbers, or characters. Dropping the second *L* while retaining the use of an *I* and two *T*s kept it closer to the actual spelling of the movie title than dropping the second *T*.

Bullitt's Chargers are more correctly MIA. Given the power of social media and the fact that both of the Bullitt movie Mustangs have survived and recently surfaced, there is little doubt that someday, somehow, the VIN numbers of the two original Chargers will surface along with the whereabouts or fate of the surviving Bullitt Dodge.

The car was ultimately parked for mechanical needs around 1980 and then followed the family as it relocated from New Jersey to Kentucky, and then on to Tennessee at the Kiernan family's horse farm. By this time, the clutch was shot, a few parts went missing along the way, and the car sat in quiet retirement. Robert Kiernan Sr. died in 2014. The car was never truly lost, yet completely out of the public eye. From the mid-1970s until 2018, it sat in very private repose.

At this point, the rumor mill went crazy prognosticating its fate. There was speculation that it had been totaled. Another rumor claimed that it had suffered a minor accident, damaging one of the front fenders. A common thread was that the owners were hoarders and hermits who were protected by shotguns and rabid dogs and wanted to keep the car a secret. Few imagined or investigated the possi-

bility that the Kiernan family was still in possession of the car.

Much more to come.

The waters surrounding the remaining Dodge Charger are considerably murkier. Of course, one of the cars was burned up in the final, fiery scene of the car chase. The surviving car remains missing. I went to Galen Govier, the ultimate source when it comes to Chrysler Corporation VINs, serial number and VIN tags, build sheets, and other evidences of Chrysler/Dodge/Plymouth muscle car provenance. He's the namesake and driving force behind Galen's Tag Service, LLC. Govier doesn't have the VIN for either of the two cars that were purchased at a Southern California Dodge dealer prior to filming. Nor does Frank A. Panacci, Anthony Bologna, Glen Kalmack, nor any other of the noted *Bullitt* movie and vehicle experts. Govier recounts an instance where he was asked to validate a

Charger that the owner claimed was the remaining *Bullitt* Dodge. The owner or owner's representative with the engineless car made all sorts of claims and representations as to why this car was the real deal but couldn't produce any paperwork to document the claim. The car appeared to have holes drilled in various areas of the chassis purportedly to accommodate camera mounting rigs and cables and wires, but those could have been drilled by anyone at any time. Without any bill of sale paperwork to prove when and where the cars were bought (or if it was bought by Warner Brothers or Solar Productions), Govier wasn't able to authenticate the car's connection to the film or to the production.

As of this writing, the location and even the existence of the missing-link Charger is entirely in question. If you have it, and the paperwork to prove it, let me know, as it would be a big piece of the *Bullitt* puzzle and big news in the autosphere, for sure.

Bullitt Mustang Stunt Car
Lost and Found

Miraculously, the stunt/jumper Mustang chassis 558 missed its date with a wrecking-yard crusher. How this happened is unclear, and no documentation about it has ever surfaced, but somehow the car stayed whole and ended up in Mexico. Its post-*Bullitt* ownership trail isn't well documented, but it was believed to have been driven regularly for three to four years once in Mexico based on licensing stickers found with the car. It's hard to imagine that such an historic and famous car was hiding in plain sight for 40-some years, although it's doubtful that any owner in Mexico had knowledge or documentation as to the car's provenance. After all, it was painted several different colors on top of the original Highland Green Metallic.

Luckily for the car and the owner, the 558 wound up in the hands of Ralph Garcia Jr. Garcia is an intelligent, friendly, and affable man who owns custom shops

Would any knowledgeable art collector toss out an authentic Monet or Renoir? Of course not. It is highly likely, if not certain, that whoever owned and drove this hapless Mustang as an everyday driver in Mexico couldn't have known the car's true history or provenance. How it escaped a wrecking-yard crusher is unknown. (Photo Courtesy Ralph Garcia Jr. Collection)

558 Rescued! Esmerelda and Ralph Garcia Jr. pull the wraps off of their own personal Monet and Renoir, the stunt/jumper Bullitt Mustang, which has been saved and is being restored. Since Garcia owns and operates a Mustang build and restoration shop, he was a bit overwhelmed by what he'd found and was able to acquire.

specializing in resto-moding Mustangs—particularly into tributes of the famous "Eleanor" Shelby-style Mustang featured in the 2000 remake of *Gone in 60 Seconds*. Naturally, this puts him constantly on the hunt for rebuildable 1967/1968 Mustangs. Garcia maintains shops in the Inland Empire area of Southern California and Mexicali, a US/Mexico border city on the Mexico side of the line, so he draws customers and donor cars from both countries.

Ralph's life changed on November 16, 2017, for two major (if hardly comparable) reasons. The first is that his father passed away on November 16, 2016. He remembered a lot of tears and prayer on the days after his dad's death. On this sad one-year anniversary, Ralph's frequent business partner and friend, Hugo Sanchez, called

Smiles are all around as (from left) Ralph Garcia Jr., Kevin Marti, and Hugo Sanchez gather in Mexico to vet and reveal that this junkyard dog was indeed one of the two Bullitt Mustangs. Once they reviewed the Marti Auto Works build sheet report and window sticker data, Garcia and Sanchez were quite sure they knew what they had but wouldn't rest on it until Marti had seen and touched the car. (Photo Courtesy Ralph Garcia Jr. Collection)

to say he found an S-Code big-block Mustang GT fastback in someone's backyard junkyard for sale.

When building a Mustang into an Eleanor clone, Garcia often doesn't pay much attention to its original build specs, equipment, or drivetrain because most of those components and amenities are stripped away and replaced in the resto-mod process. With this car being a rare S-Code 390 V-8 car, Garcia and Sanchez decided to check with Marti Auto Works for a Marti Report, which decodes the VIN and all the other numbers and codes to determine exactly to what spec, colors, trim levels, and powertrain it had and where and when a given Mustang (or nearly any Ford, Lincoln, or Mercury between model years 1949 and 2007) was built. Marti confirmed what Sanchez suspected: the car in their sights was one of the two Mustangs used in the filming of *Bullitt*. In fact, it was identified as the stunt/jumper Mustang that performed most of the chase scene's more dangerous stunts and was written off as a total loss due to damage sustained in filming the final segments of the chase scene and destined to be crushed and destroyed but never was.

Marti, Sanchez, and Garcia immediately agreed not to build the car into an Eleanor clone for a customer. The car was in good news/bad news condition. It was whole and in one piece, offered for sale at a reasonable price, and had its VIN tag and other serial number stampings intact. However, it was rusted throughout the floors and much of the lower fenders and rocker panels, and the drivetrain was missing upon discovery.

The car was sitting in someone's backyard near Cabo San Lucas, and the owner advertised it for sale on the internet, which is how Sanchez discovered it. In as much as the two *Bullitt* Mustang VINs were well-known in the Mustang community, Garcia and Sanchez were highly confident that this was the missing stunt car. The car exhibited no evidence of any re-stamping or swapping of data plates or other VIN body stampings being manipulated, forged, or otherwise tampered with. They secured the car and already had an Eleanor build client committed to their next project.

Even though the Mustang-savvy business partners had confidence that the information disclosed in the Marti Auto Works deluxe report was accurate, they wanted to go the extra mile to make sure they had the real deal. They engaged Kevin Marti to visit the car, inspect it, and authenticate that it was legitimate *Bullitt* Mustang provenance.

Marti went to Mexico, inspected the car, and confirmed that the body, VIN tags, and stampings were legitimate, and that it was one of the two cars that Steve McQueen, Carey Loftin, and Bud Ekins

A highly patinated factory Ford VIN tag tells the story. The numbers are clear, readable, and unmodified. Marti also confirmed that the rivets holding it in place are original, thus this plate wasn't swapped in from another car or a reproduction piece. It is good as gold, or 50-year-old aluminum in this case. (Photo Courtesy Ralph Garcia Jr. Collection)

The all-important VIN stamp on the driver's side of the core support area under the hood also shows the wear and patina of the hard-living car with the all-important 558 stamping clear and unmodified. Bingo! (Photo Courtesy Ralph Garcia Jr. Collection)

Even though the areas around the engine compartment VIN stamping have been repainted in Highland Green Metallic, Garcia and his team masked off the numbers so they could be seen in a clean but unrestored and unpainted form. Smart move. (Photo Courtesy Ralph Garcia Jr. Collection)

pounded up and down and around the streets of San Francisco in 1968. Talk about striking movie car and pop culture gold!

Garcia and Sanchez were giddy about their amazing find and acquisition, so much so that they held a party for the car in Mexico, and many locals, friends, family, and Ford enthusiasts attended. The entire affair about the car made a huge social media splash as well, which caused an amazing number of people to question the car's legitimacy. This is somewhat understandable because the stunt/jumper was presumed to be crushed and destroyed decades prior, and the idea that it had somehow escaped that fate, made it to Mexico, survived, and ended up in the hands of a Mustang restoration business owner was a little far-fetched for some. Garcia quietly held his ground and

made plans for the car's restoration. He had the world's top authority on Mustang build sheets, window stickers, and serial numbers in his corner, with Kevin Marti having personally vetted and subsequently authenticated the car. After a while, the conspiracy theorists went quiet, and Garcia and Sanchez went to work.

Given the car's substantial rust damage, multiple coats of paint, and neglected interior, there was little question that the car needed and deserved a complete restoration with a careful eye toward preserving any remaining originality. Garcia and Sanchez assembled a team to coach and consult on how to approach restoring the car. They included automotive aftermarket marketing specialist Jeff Cater, Marti, aforementioned *Bullitt* Mustang guru Glen Kalmack, and others. Work began in Garcia's

Sadly the 558's cabin was pretty thrashed from years of abuse and sitting abandoned in a backyard junkyard. The Shelby steering wheel was long gone, as was much of the dash trim, although these seats are likely original and came with the car. Fortunately, all of the interior trim specs are known, so restoring it to Bullitt movie car spec won't be all that mysterious.

The 558's rear seat area shows some extra holes and metalwork created to handle camera, lighting, and mic mounts. Fortunately, all of the evidence of this provenance has remained largely untouched. Of course, in the restoration, Garcia and Team 558 will fully protect and preserve any movie car mods made to the Mustang. It is more than a bit lucky that the lower chassis and body panel rust this car suffered didn't affect this area of the car in any meaningful way.

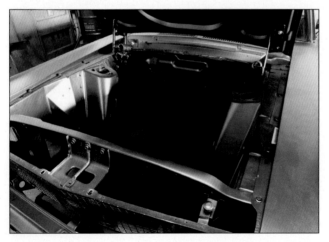

Something big is missing here: 390 cubic inches worth of Ford FE big-block V-8 and its attendant Top Loader 4-speed transmission. The original transmission is MIA, but the original numbers-matching engine block has been located and the 558's owners are working hard to secure it. If they can't, a proper date-code-correct powertrain has also been sourced and will be installed.

This look at the trunk area shows a plethora of the holes that were drilled inside the car to accommodate all sorts of wiring for cameras, lights, and mics. Zoom in and you'll see the "smokestack" used for an onboard generator needed to power all the equipment.

shop in Mexicali, whereas much of the original sheet metal as possible was preserved. The areas deemed unsavable, such as the rocker panels, floors, and bottom areas of the fenders, were replaced with as much new old stock (NOS) sheet metal as they could locate or with new reproduction patch panels as needed. Fortunately, none of the metal that required replacing was stamped with the VIN of this car. However, it is still a shame that many of the body panels had simply rusted into hamburger and couldn't be saved.

Look just below the edge of the gas tank and you'll see another staggered row of holes drilled to accommodate sound, light, and camera wiring. Thank goodness no one used filler or welded up these holes along the way.

That said, a surprising number of original and modified equipment and panels remained. Along the trail of the previous five decades, the mounting points and hardware for some of the camera and sound equipment mounts had been torched off the bottom of the car, so those modifications were gone. Yet somehow the lower rear fascia panel with evidence of the removal of the rear backup lights had survived in rough shape but was deemed restorable.

Some of the best physical evidence (besides the number plates and VIN stampings) of the car's considerable provenance survived in the trunk area, which was riddled with holes drilled for the running of microphone, camera, and other electrical wires. Fortunately, in all of the 558's subsequent paint jobs, all of these holes were never patched or filled in. And amazingly, the small sheet metal smokestack that pumped oil smoke out over the rear axle to accentuate the smokiness of the countless burnouts the car performed in the film also survived and stayed in the trunk safe and sound.

The biggest missing pieces of the puzzle were the original 390 V-8 engine and Ford Top Loader 4-speed transmission. Garcia and team went about sourcing an

"Life's a GAS for 558!" For a time, the 558 Mustang checked into the famous Galpin Auto Sports (GAS) for some expert restoration work. If anyone knows how to restore a Mustang this special, it would be the custom shop owned and operated by what was the world's number one–selling Ford dealership for nearly three decades.

Galpin's Mad Mike takes a look under the hood as the 558 Mustang rolls into the GAS resto and mod shop. Galpin COO Beau Boeckmann is standing behind the car next to the driver's door, and Ralph Garcia Jr. can be partially seen behind the edge of the hood near the left front fender.

It was actually an unplanned coincidence that a resto-moded black Dodge Charger happened to be in the GAS shop just as the Bullitt Mustang 558 arrived. Note the Dodge's "FELON" license plate. Perhaps the car's owner thought this choice was safer than "HITMEN."

Upon arrival, the GAS team jumped all over and under the Mustang to determine what had been done and what work remained to make the car 1968 Bullitt "set ready." It is a bit of a shame that some purists in the Bullittsphere tend to marginalize this car for not yet having its original numbers-matching engine, or for the need of such extensive restoration, which is absolutely unfortunate. It's true it is not as deeply original as the 559 hero/beauty machine, history cannot be recanted, and the 558 was absolutely as much a part of the production of Bullitt as was the 559 Mustang. In fact, if you count minutes on screen, the reality is that 558 did much of the heavy lifting and was featured in most of the crashing, flying, banging, and tires burning out passages.

Proud papa Ralph Garcia Jr. is shown with the 558 in his spray booth. It took more than a single attempt to get the mix and toning of the 1968 Highland Green Metallic paint just right. (Photo Courtesy Ralph Garcia Jr. Collection)

original date-code-correct 390-ci big-block Ford engine, and also a period-correct spec transmission, which they located and acquired. The partners were subsequently notified that a party known to the seller of the car had possession of the original powertrain. Negotiations began to acquire the factory engine and trans, but as of this writing, they have yet to bear fruit. Garcia said, "We need to inspect the components and make sure that the numbers match and indicate it is in fact the engine and transmission that this car was born with, and of course that they are in sound and complete-enough condition to be properly restored."

As of this writing, the parties have not yet agreed on how to manage the inspection process, nor have they agreed on pricing. "But, the right place for that engine is in this car," Garcia added, and he seems highly committed to acquiring it.

A good portion of the early restoration work was done in Garcia's Mexicali shop, and then it was moved to his California facility. Late in 2018, in the interest of an absolutely correct concours-quality restoration, Garcia and company decided to turn the car over to Galpin Auto Sports (GAS), the restoration and build shop belonging to legendary Galpin Motors in the San Fernando Valley area of Southern California, just over the Hollywood Hills from Los Angeles. The car was transported from Garcia's shop to GAS in January 2019.

At this point, there was considerable debate and discussion about to what point in time and to which condition the car should be restored. There was no question it would be restored to *Bullitt* movie car specifications with all of the equipment and modifications that made it film- and stunt-ready. But many detailed questions remained: should the paint be finished to shiny, new car standards or dulled down with cleanser and dented up a bit as it was finished in Lee Brown's body shop in 1968. Should the camera mounts and such be recreated and installed beneath the car? The GAS team was clear about the fact that the Highland Green Metallic, as sprayed by Garcia's shop, was slightly off-hue to the original Ford paint spec so the car would need to be repainted. As of this writing, all of these issues are still being debated. For a variety of reasons, Garcia and Galpin agreed that Garcia should take the car back into his own shop for the balance of the restoration and finishing. This happened in the late spring of 2019, and the final work and specification of the restoration remains in final process as of early 2020.

As the 558 team set about the path of bringing the Mexico Mustang back to life and glory, several other questions remained unanswered: What of the other car (the chassis 559 hero or beauty car)? Where is it? What condition is it in? Would it also soon surface?

FOR PEOPLE WHO LOVE CARS ®

HAGERTY

JANUARY | FEBRUARY 2018 // HAGERTY.COM

MCQUEEN'S MUSTANG
FOUND AT LAST

The Kiernans' 559 hero/beauty Mustang stars on the cover of Hagerty Insurance Company's enthusiast magazine, which helped break the story of how the car went into quiet semi-retirement and how it surfaced back into the public eye. (Photo Courtesy Hagerty)

The answer that the *Bullitt* and Mustang worlds awaited was delivered in early 2018. Despite the rumors, lies, innuendo, and misinformation, the Kiernan family still owned the car. It was living in quiet repose at the family's horse farm in Tennessee. Robert Kiernan's son Sean told the story to Hagerty Insurance Company, which reported it in its enthusiast magazine.

"The Bullitt was, at this point, in pieces. In 2001, right about the time Bob Kiernan retired, Ford introduced a Bullitt [edition] Mustang GT. That, plus Bob's newfound free time, sparked a plan between father and son to get their car back on the road. 'We didn't want to keep

Freshened up mechanically but not made falsely shiny, the 559 Bullitt Mustang is deeply original: scars, warts, and all. Nearly everything you can see here is factory and/or Bullitt film set original, with the exception of the tires. (Photo Courtesy Ford Motor Company)

it from the public,' Sean said, 'but the attention over the years was annoying.' Nevertheless, they agreed the time had come to share their treasure.

"Now 33 years old and with a bad clutch, the Bullitt was tired. 'We planned to do just enough to make it drivable. We didn't want to touch the history,' said Sean. They took it apart, but then, Sean said, 'Life happened.' Bob was diagnosed with Parkinson's disease. Sean got married and had a kid. And the Mustang sat in pieces.

"Hollywood had, in the meantime, come calling again. Just before the Mustang was parked, a producer for the movie *Charlie's Angels* wrote and said that one of the stars (Drew Barrymore) desperately wanted the original car for the film. Bob again told Hollywood to stuff it. 'It wasn't about the money,' Sean said. 'My dad wasn't stubborn; he just loved the thing. He wanted it in his garage forever.'

Sean added with pride, 'My dad [effectively] told Steve McQueen thanks but no thanks.'

"When Ford introduced a second Bullitt Mustang [tribute model] in 2008, that sparked the pair to have the engine rebuilt. Again, things got in the way. Sean had a second kid and then got divorced in 2009. His father's Parkinson's worsened, and keeping the farm going and the horses fed simply took more time. The Bullitt project stalled, but there was never a thought of punching out and selling. 'We knew we'd get to it,' Sean said.

"Sadly, they never did. In 2014 . . . Bob unexpectedly died. The responsibilities of the father fell to the son. Sean, who had remarried, suddenly had a farm and his mom to care for. 'We moved into my dad's house,' he said, 'out in the sticks.' He remembered sitting on a step in the garage and staring at the pile of Mustang parts as he wondered, with some dread, 'What am

The look is aggressive, the stance is perfect, and the patina is as real as the sun and the moon. It's just exactly what Steve McQueen wanted for Lt. Frank Bullitt. A star was reborn! Thankfully, Sean Kiernan knew to leave well enough alone. (Photo Courtesy Ford Motor Company)

Rust, scrapes, missing paint, wide tires, blacked out trim, and straight cut single exhaust pipes is the look defined by the Bullitt Mustangs. (Photo Courtesy Ford Motor Company)

The original GT emblem on this gas cap was removed in 1968 and the center of the cap was not so carefully painted flat black. This is what's left of that original bit of paint applied at Lee Brown's body shop in 1968. (Photo Courtesy Ford Motor Company)

The original Shelby GT500 steering wheel was missing, but fortunately, highly authentic-looking reproduction pieces are available in the aftermarket. It's now replaced and looking just right. (Photo Courtesy Ford Motor Company)

The 559's original 8,000-rpm tach remains. Note the remnants of some tape residue on the right side of the gauge intended to mark off a redline of around 6,000 rpm, as if Ekins, McQueen, and the other drivers were going to pay this any mind. Burnouts were more important than damaging the engines of the hard-driven movie cars. (Photo Courtesy Ford Motor Company)

This original lower-rear fascia panel shows clear evidence that the backup lamps have been removed and the holes have been filled. The 558 stunt car also shares this detail. (Photo Courtesy Ford Motor Company)

Another important VIN tag on 559 is located at the base of the windshield. In this case it is fully intact and with all the correct numbers as yet another layer of proof as to the car's originality. Note the 1980 New Jersey state registration sticker just above a Warner Brothers-Seven Arts parking sticker. The 559 exhibits provenance to spare and in spades enough to satisfy anyone looking to vet or authenticate this museum piece. (Photo Courtesy Ford Motor Company)

Now that's one hard-working American Torq Thrust wheel. The blacked-out center spokes are faded, chipped, and corroded; and the wheel lip lost its polished luster long ago. Note that the center hubcap is held on with fewer than five screws. (Photo Courtesy Ford Motor Company)

This door tag is the first place that Kevin Marti looked once he was face-to-face with the car. It told the entire story: this was the real Bullitt *Mustang. Every number, every stamping, and every code matched the factory build paperwork perfectly. Without question it confirmed what the Kiernan family had known all along. It was the long-thought-missing McQueen machine. (Photo Courtesy Ford Motor Company)*

I going to do with the car?'

"'I can build a show car all day long,' he said, 'but this was history. What if I screwed it up? The Bullitt scared the shit out of me.' None of them had the money to bring in a professional who was used to curating an artifact. The lucky break was that Sean and his dad had left the body largely untouched. They hadn't removed the doors or the dash. Everything was there. So during the first five months of 2016, Sean carefully put it back together in his father's small garage."

Fortunately, Sean had the good sense to only mechanically recommission (or sympathetically restore) the famous Mustang and not to restore it in the classic sense of exploding it down the chassis and cosmetically restoring and refinishing every surface and component. Kiernan wisely resisted the temptation to make it new. Instead, he only freshened the car mechanically so that it was drivable and safe to be driven while leaving in place its physical and visual stories in the form of dulled paint, surface-rusted chrome, dents, dings, scrapes, age, and wear that it endured during the filming of *Bullitt*

and in the ensuing nearly five decades of dormancy. This included refreshing the engine, clutch, transmission, belts, hoses, fluids, and brakes to make the car a legitimate runner, yet preserving nearly every visible finish and surface possible that demonstrates its deep originality.

Sean Kiernan said that it was time to share the car. This would have been exciting even if it were fully assembled as a non-running car, but of course the message is so much more compelling with it not only looking but also sounding and moving as it did with Steve McQueen at the wheel in 1968—with every sticker, piece of tape, and blemish earned along the *Bullitt* trail intact. Brilliant!

Not wishing to leave a single detail to chance, Kiernan wanted authoritative third-party confirmation of what he already knew from firsthand experience: that his car, Mustang 559, was in fact the hero/beauty car used in the filming of *Bullitt*. Fortunately the ownership chain was well known with immaculate paperwork from Warner Brothers Studios through subsequent owners to his father, Robert Kiernan. Like Garcia, he also engaged

Marti Auto Works to vet and authenticate the car that had been in his real and metaphorical garage since his father purchased the car in the 1970s. Kevin Marti flew out, visited the car, and provided both copies of the original dealer window sticker data and all of the build sheet information to confirm the car's build dates, locale, spec, and equipment. Marti verified the car's originality and that all of the VIN tags and stamps were unimpeachably authentic, as was the rest of the car.

Marti was blown away, the Haggerty article continued.

"'I walked in to see the car,' he said, 'and thought, 'Here's another car that looks like the Bullitt.' I went over, looked at the VIN on the tag, and immediately, my emotions flipped from skepticism to 'Oh, my god, it's real.'

"Marti marveled at the modifications made for the movie. Underneath the rockers, three metal tubes were clumsily welded perpendicular to the car's center line for camera mounts. There were holes cut in the trunk for the cords that ran from a generator to power the cameras and lights. Even tape residue remained—on the tachometer to mark the redline, and on the floor, presumably to secure the seat belts and wires. 'Ninety-eight percent of the original car is there,' he said. 'It's an incredible artifact.'"

The holy grail of Mustangs, 558 and 559, indeed survived and surfaced.

The tally of the most significant movie star cars from *Bullitt* is Mustang: 2, Charger: 0. Both of the Mustangs used in the making of the film have survived with their whereabouts known and documentation confirmed. Charger fans aren't as lucky. One of the movie's stunt cars was confirmed to be destroyed during production, and the second car's whereabouts, survival, and VIN are unknown.

The 559 Joins the Historic Vehicle Register

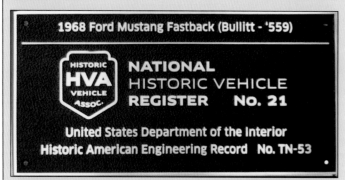

1968 Ford Mustang Fastback (Bullitt - '559)

HISTORIC **HVA** VEHICLE ASSOC.

NATIONAL HISTORIC VEHICLE REGISTER NO. 21

United States Department of the Interior
Historic American Engineering Record No. TN-53

The license plate–sized and –shaped bronze plaque from the Historical Vehicle Association commemorates the 559's place in the Historic Vehicle Register and the Library of Congress. (Photo Courtesy Ford Motor Company)

As an ultimate and final verification of its authenticity and provenance, the Kiernans's 559 *Bullitt* Mustang was inducted into the Historic Vehicle Register by the Historic Vehicle Association (HVA). The mission of the HVA is to promote the cultural and historical significance of the automobile and protect the future of our automotive past. The HVA is a joint venture between itself as the primary research and documentary organization, Hagerty Insurance Company, and the Library of Congress.

The Organization Aims to Achieve This Mission By:
1. Documenting and recognizing historically important vehicles in a National Historic Vehicle Register (HVR).
2. Establishing and sharing best-practice guidelines to ensure that authentic examples of our automotive past will be available for future generations.
3. Promoting the historical and cultural significance of the automobile through media and events.
4. Protecting the future of our automotive past through affiliations with museums and academic institutions, educational programs, and support of legislative action.

Through the collective efforts of enthusiasts, specialists, and professionals, the HVA aims to ensure that our automotive heritage is more broadly appreciated and carefully preserved for future generations.

With over 375,000 members, the HVA is the world's largest historic vehicle owners' organization. The HVA was founded in 2009 through the philanthropic support of Hagerty and became the designated North American representative of Fédération International des Véhicules Anciens (FIVA), the international federation of historic vehicle organizations.

The certification and documentation processes are grueling to say the least. The HVA has established a laboratory, photo studio, and documentation research facility in Allentown, Pennsylvania, staffed by researchers, scientists, and digital photography and imaging experts who can test and document any vehicle to determine the authenticity of metal, identification plates, serial number stampings, rubber, and a variety of other parameters. Only those vehicles determined to pass the strictest tests of authenticity and historical significance are inducted into the HVR, which then makes all

of the HVA documentation part of the Library of Congress. The HVR only inducts a handful of vehicles each year, and many of them are one-offs, prototypes, and singularly significant vehicles to transportation history.

The guidelines for consideration for the National HVR have been created in conjunction with the Department of the Interior. This program is a work in progress and specific language will continue to be refined and developed over the course of the coming years. Each of the initial vehicles will help to act as a case study to perfect the process of nominating, documenting, and collecting vehicles and their histories and specifications.

It is vastly significant on many levels that the HVA elected to vet the 559 *Bullitt* Mustang and induct it into the HVR in 2019. Besides all of the vetting, testing, research, and documentation, something that makes this recognition so significant is that each vehicle is encased in a specially constructed glass jewel box and displayed on the National Mall in Washington, DC, for a week. This recognizes the vehicle's official recognition by the Library of Congress and shares the car with locals and tourists

The 559 is all boxed up and ready for display on the National Mall, between the Congressional buildings and the Washington Monument in Washington, DC. All of the cars inducted into the Historic Vehicle Register earn this honor, and the displays are open to the public and free of charge. (Photo Courtesy Ford Motor Company)

alike, 24/7, at no cost. The full-car-sized glass display case is beautifully lit, and with a variety of DC's most significant buildings and monuments clearly visible in the background, the visuals are stunning to say the least.

What other sorts of vehicles have been recognized equally with the 559 *Bullitt* Mustang? Check out the following list, and you'll further understand the depth of this recognition for this particular car, and for *Bullitt*'s significance in pop culture and film history.

From HVA Registry, including the Historic American Engineering Record (HAER) number:

- 1964 Shelby Cobra Daytona Coupe CSX2287, HAER number: PA-650
- 1964 Meyers Manx *Old Red*, HAER number: CA-2312
- 1938 Maserati 8CTF *The Boyle Special*, HAER number: IN-112
- 1918 Cadillac U.S. 1257X, HAER number: WA-225
- 1947 Tucker 48 Prototype *The Tin Goose*, HAER Number: PA-652
- 1940 GM Futurliner No. 10, HAER number: IN-114
- 1954 Mercedes-Benz 300 SL, HAER number: PA-194
- 1940 Ford Pilot Model GP-NO.1 (PYGMY), HAER number: AL-213
- 1909 White Model M Steam Car, HAER number: MA-175
- 1962 Willys Jeep Universal Model CJ-6, HAER number: CA-2320
- 1911 Marmon Wasp, HAER number: IN-115
- 1907 Thomas Flyer, HAER number: NV-49
- 1920 Anderson Six, HAER number: SC-44
- Buick Y-Job, HAER number: MI-417
- 1967 Chevrolet Camaro, HAER number: KS-11
- 1932 Ford V-8 Roadster *McGee Roadster*, HAER number: CA-2327
- 1951 Mercury Sport Coupe *Hirohata Merc*, HAER number: CA-2328
- 1964 Chevrolet Impala *Gypsy Rose*, HAER number: CA-2329
- 1933 Graham 8 Sedan *Blue Streak*, HAER number: PA-654
- 1896 Benton Harbor Motor Carriage, HAER number: PA-655
- 1968 Ford Mustang Fastback (*Bullitt* 559), HAER number: TN-53
- 1985 Modena Spyder *Ferris Bueller* Ferrari, HAER number: MD-192
- 1927 Ford Model T Touring *15 Millionth Ford*, HAER number: MI-419
- 1984 Plymouth *Voyager Magic Wagon No. 1*, HAER number: MI-420
- 1969 Chevrolet Corvette Stingray driven by Alan Bean, the fourth person to walk on the moon) HAER number: TX-3404[8]

The view of Historic Vehicle Register inductees opposite the halls of Congress is particularly compelling at night. Many of the world's most historically significant and valuable vehicles have earned this particular honor, and the Bullitt Mustang absolutely belongs among them for its automotive, cinematic, and cultural significance. (Photo Courtesy Ford Motor Company)

Chapter 6

BULLITT *RELOADED*
FORD'S TRIBUTE BULLITT
EDITION MUSTANGS

This amazing Ford design concept illustration, dated 1999, tells us that Ford was at least toying with the idea of a new-generation Bullitt edition Mustang at least a year before the full-sized concept was first shown at the LA Auto Show. This illustration came very close to how the final production version looked. The similarities in terms of colors and wheels are obvious, but even the details differ in only a few small ways. The production version had open vent holes, sans any lights, and this sketch shows foglights in the lower front fascia. The final 2001 design also had blacked-out GT badges on aft portions of the front fenders. Otherwise, this design concept looks nearly production ready about two years before the car hit the streets. (Photo Courtesy Ford Motor Company)

At the 2000 Los Angeles Auto Show, Ford unveiled a Bullitt Edition Concept Mustang. It was built on the then-current Mustang GT coupe bodystyle, stripped of most of its badging and chrome trim, painted Dark Highland Green, and featured wheels reminiscent of the Amer-ican Racing Torq Thrust D wheels run on the 1968 movie Mustangs. Despite how this particular bodystyle didn't resemble the 1968 GT390 fastback very much, it looked great, and the metaphors were more than credible.

On the show floor, I asked Ford's

then-global vice-president of design, J Mays, about the story behind the new Bullitt. He said, "No two guys, outside of Ford, have done more for the Mustang than Carroll Shelby and Steve McQueen." The Carroll Shelby reference was logical enough, considering the seminal Shelby GT350 and GT500 Mustangs produced by Shelby American from 1965–1970. The Steve McQueen reference was equally obvious, with the Mustang's role as one of the stars of *Bullitt*. I asked Mays if Ford planned to produce a limited-edition Mustang Bullitt tribute model that resembled the concept car on the show floor. His answer was careful but telling. "At this moment, we've announced no plan to do such a thing," he said. "But we could." And Ford did just that a few months after that acclaimed LA Auto Show reveal.

Based on the 2001 Mustang GT, the limited-production Bullitt featured a 4.6-liter V-8 tweaked for better airflow with a modest power increase (from 260 to 265 hp), including a cast-aluminum intake, twin 57-mm bore throttle bodies, and high-flow mufflers.

Team Mustang also gave the Bullitt a firmer lowered suspension for tighter handling as well as special exterior enhancements and interior touches meant to capture the spirit of the movie car. Unique wheels, "Bullitt" badging, and a brushed-aluminum fuel-filler door helped complete the look with a factory serialized identification label included to verify each 2001 Bullitt.

Surprise! Or not. Jim O'Conner, president of Ford at the time, announced on January 4, 2001, that Ford would build and sell a production version of the Bullitt concept vehicle that was shown the year prior. Fortunately, the car lost virtually nothing in translation from turntable toy to production vehicle. The look and the specs were just right. (Photo Courtesy Ford Motor Company)

In 2001, the Bullitt was truly new again. San Francisco's remarkable skyline, Dave Kunz's wonderful 1968 Bullitt Mustang tribute car, and the first official Ford tribute model to Bullitt since the original cars from 1968: the 2001 Ford Mustang Bullitt Edition. (Photo Courtesy Ford Motor Company)

Of course, the original movie cars were purposefully stripped of all badging and model identification, but Ford rightly concluded that a new Bullitt Edition tribute model must have some indicator, other than Highland Green Metallic paint, to let everyone know of the car's heritage and provenance. This simple tail panel badge did the job nicely. (Photo Courtesy Ford Motor Company)

The 2001 Bullitt cabin was simple, primarily black, and to the point. There was no wood trim as on the movie cars, as Ford didn't offer it on the Mustang at the time and rightly decided it wasn't mission-critical on this limited-edition model. The look was clean and businesslike, much like the original. (Photo Courtesy Ford Motor Company)

One design touch given to the 2001 Mustang Bullitt is this satin aluminum–finished fuel-door cover. We find this a slightly odd design choice as it doesn't have any direct connection to the look of the movie cars, which of course used a chrome gas cap on the upper rear fascia taillight panel. And besides, the film cars were specifically costumed for less flash and less bling. No matter, it's a nice-looking piece on the modern car, even if there's not a strong connection to the original.

One bit of special flash granted to the 2001 Mustang Bullitt's cabin that was unique to this model was the brushed aluminum (not plastic) shift knob. It is different than what was on the movie cars, but we suspect McQueen would have liked it. (Photo Courtesy Ford Motor Company)

The specs are as follows:

Engine
Type: 90-degree SOHC 16-valve V-8
Displacement: 4.6L (281 ci)
Horsepower: 265 at 5,000 rpm
Torque: 305 ft-lbs at 4,000 rpm
Bore x Stroke: 90.2 mm x 90 mm
Compression: 9.4:1

Suspension
Front: Modified MacPherson strut (Tokiko), stabilizer bar, coil springs, lowered 0.75 inch.

Rear: Solid axle, 4-link locating arms, coil springs, sub-frame connectors, lowered 0.75 inch.

Brakes
Front: 13.0 inch. vented Brembo disc, PBR twin-piston caliper (painted red)
Rear: 11.65 inch. vented disc, single-piston caliper
ABS: Four-channel ABS system, linked to all-speed traction control

Wheels
Wheels: 17 x 8 inch 5-spoke American

Another alloy splash in the 2001 Bullitt's interior is the rubber-studded, brushed-aluminum pedals. The look is clean, racy, and the rubber studs grab the driver's shoes for good control, perhaps when bounding up and down the hilly streets of San Francisco. (Photo Courtesy Ford Motor Company)

Even though the original movie cars had no sill plate identification that was given to the 2001 Ford Bullitt model, it's a handsome touch to remind the owner and anyone else who enters the car that they are aboard something special. (Photo Courtesy Ford Motor Company)

It wouldn't be a Bullitt Mustang without American Racing Torq Thrust D-style wheels. The ones Ford put on the 2001 Bullitt looked just right—aside from the spoke finish. Although it was handsome and elegant from a design standpoint, it was lighter and more reflective than the matte-black finish on the movie cars' wheel spokes. Also, notice that the fenders kept their GT, instead of 4.6 engine, badges that were shorn from the movie cars. This gen didn't have a 5.0 option. However, it all worked. (Photo Courtesy Ford Motor Company)

See, new Mustangs can jump. It wouldn't be a Bullitt Mustang (later renamed Mustang Bullitt) if it didn't fly through the streets of San Francisco every now and again, so Ford did the deed for the cameras and because they could. We're not aware of any oil pans that were injured in the making of this photo. (Photo Courtesy Ford Motor Company)

A bit of splash that Ford added to the 2001 Mustang Bullitt was the racing red brake calipers, which was something not seen on the original movie cars. However, this visual touch was well received. Porsche, Ferrari, and other carmakers had made variously hued painted calipers a popular performance visual touch by this time. (Photo Courtesy Ford Motor Company)

Racing Torq Thrust forged aluminum
Tires: 245/45R-17 BSW Goodyear Eagle

Performance
0 to 60 mph: 5.6 seconds
60 to 0 braking: 118 feet
1/4-mile: 14.0 seconds at 97.9 mph

A concession the product team made in the name of marketing considerations was that not everyone wanted a green Mustang. The car was offered in a choice of three colors: Dark Highland Green, True Blue, and black. The car proved handsome in both of the additional colors, although the *Bullitt* faithful scoffed (somewhat legitimately) that it just wasn't a *Bullitt* Mustang if it wasn't painted Highland Green. This proved to be the case in the sales and production numbers as well: the Dark Highland Green paint selection was the most popular with 3,041 units produced, black was second with 1,819 units produced, and True Blue was the distant runner up with just 722 cars produced. In all, 5,582 2001 Ford Bullitt Edition Mustangs were produced.

This photo shows that the 2001's version of Dark Highland Green, especially in the afternoon sun, is slightly warmer than the 1968 recipe. However, it's a great look, and looks much more like the earlier original hue when it's in the shade or darker light. (Photo Courtesy Ford Motor Company)

Sans front foglights and much of its chrome trim but with extra performance, the 2001 Mustang Bullitt Edition not only talked the talk but credibly walked the walk. The only things missing on this Ford Motor Company studio photo are the GT badges on the fenders. Otherwise it's showroom ready. Some collectors prefer this original Ford-produced Bullitt commemorative car to any of the later versions. What worked in 1968 certainly worked in 2001. (Photo Courtesy Ford Motor Company)

Some call him the "Son of Cool," which is fair game. A casual and obviously pleased Chad McQueen joins Ford in its San Francisco media presentation and drive program for the first new-gen Bullitt Mustang from Ford. Just behind him and the car, standing up against the diner wall in a blue blazer with his arms crossed, is Chris Theodore, the now-retired Ford product planning chief, who was responsible for several Shelby concept cars and the production of the 2003–2005 Ford GT. (Photo Courtesy Ford Motor Company)

2008/2009 Ford Mustang Bullitt Editions

A press release from performance.ford.com sums up the 2008 Ford Mustang Bullitt Edition:

"Shortly after the all-new 2005 Mustang was launched, talk of reintroducing a Bullitt edition was rampant among Mustang enthusiasts. With the sheet metal atop the new S-197 platform so closely mirroring the classic 1968 Mustang shape, it's no wonder that so many people were excited when Ford unveiled the Bullitt edition Mustang GT for 2008, which neatly recognized and celebrated the 40th anniversary of the making of the film.

"Engineers tapped Ford Racing for a host of upgrades to make the new Bullitt much more than just an appearance package. Ford Racing's Power Upgrade Package added 15 extra hp to the Mustang GT's 300 ponies. Suspension tweaks included stiffer shocks, springs, and a strut tower brace, giving the Bullitt extra bite in the corners. Bullitt-specific front brake pads and 3.73 rear gears rounded out the mechanical upgrades, save for a true dual-exhaust system that was specifically tuned to sound more like Detective Frank Bullitt's own 1968 Mustang movie car.

"In keeping with the classic film, the 2008 Bullitt was stripped of badging, scoops, and spoilers with the faux gas cap on the trunk bearing the only name of this special model. A unique blacked-out grille, sans running horse and corral, and special 5-spoke 18-inch wheels finished the exterior treatments, while Bullitt-specific interior trim with Bullitt badging and an aluminum shift knob completed the Bullitt

Prior to releasing actual photos of the 2008 Mustang Bullitt Edition that everyone wanted and predicted, Ford snuck out this shadowy design rendering of what the new car might look like. "Hmmm . . . Green Mustang with a blacked-out grille, and no horse and corral emblems in that grille. Whatever could it be?" The car was highly anticipated primarily due to the new-for-2005 generation Mustang fastback coupe that looked so much more like a 1968 Mustang. The new car's performance (more than 300 hp) exceeded that of the 2001 Bullitt Mustang, and 2008 marked the 40th anniversary of Bullitt, which also added to the excitement. (Photo Courtesy Ford Motor Company)

Once the second-generation Mustang Bullitt hit the streets of San Francisco, it was obvious that the new look paid a better tribute to the original movie cars and wore the Highland Green and the five-spoke mags even more authentically than the 2001 model. (Photo Courtesy Ford Motor Company)

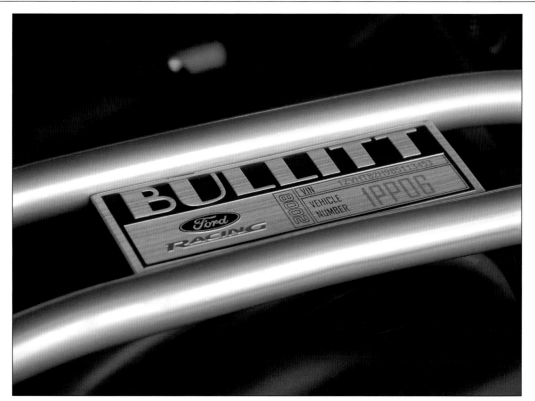

Ford Racing cleverly put each 2008/2009 Mustang Bullitt's VIN on the lightweight strut tower brace in the engine compartment.

Model-specific brushed-aluminum sill plates clearly identified each example. It's a splash of flash but still subtle. Nice touch.

Some of the interior touches developed for the 2001 Mustang Bullitt were carried over into the 2008/2009 model, particularly the aluminum shift knob, bright-trimmed shifter bezel, rubber-studded pedal pads, plus the businesslike charcoal gray cabin. Note the Bullitt logo in the middle of the steering-wheel Boss airbag.

Ford could have just as easily repurposed the Bullitt badge designed for the 2001 model, but instead it came up with this particularly clever and handsome way to ID the car by using the faux gas cap. It was more attractive and certainly a bit less stealth than the blacked-out version on the movie cars. But it was most necessary from a marketing standpoint. Nice piece, great look, good idea.

Part of the second-gen Bullitt's exhaust system included racier-sounding mufflers plus these brushed-stainless resonator exhaust tips. They were not as loud as 1968, but the effect was convincing.

Ford relied on modest and straightforward hot-rodding techniques to crank an extra measure of performance out of the 2008/2009 Bullitt's 4.6L SOHC V-8 to give it 317 hp to the stock GT's 300. These mods (developed primarily for the 2007 Ford Shelby GT Mustang) include a Ford Racing cold air intake system, a slightly more aggressive engine management system tune, a stouter 3.73:1 rear differential ratio, and a freer-breathing and throatier-sounding exhaust system. The new Bullitt looked and sounded the part, happily ripping out 5.0-second 0–60 mph runs all day.

transformation. Each 2008 Bullitt was assigned its own VIN-specific serial number on a special ID plate affixed to the car's strut tower brace. Available in either Dark Highland Green (specific to the Bullitt edition) or simply Black."

Engine
Type: 90-degree SOHC 24-valve V-8
Displacement: 4.6L (281 ci)
Horsepower: 315 at 6,000 rpm
Torque: 325 ft-lbs at 4,250 rpm
Bore x Stroke: 90.2 mm x 90 mm
Compression: 9.8:1

Suspension
Front: Reverse-L Independent MacPherson strut, stabilizer bar, Ford Racing strut tower brace
Rear: 3-link solid axle with coil springs, panhard rod, stabilizer bar

Brakes
Front: 12.4 inch vented disc, dual-piston caliper, high-performance pad

Rear: 11.8 inch vented disc, single-piston caliper
ABS: Four-channel ABS system, linked to all-speed traction control

For 2008, Ford developed its own 18-inch, five-spoke alloy wheel design that credibly aped the old American Racing mags. They were now finished in a darker, richer metallic charcoal for Bullitt duty, and they ultimately resembled the rims on the movie cars even more than the previous models.

Wheels

Wheels: 18 x 8 inch 5-spoke cast-aluminum Euroflange wheels, finished in Argent Grey

Tires: 235/50ZR-18 BSW high-performance

Performance

0 to 60 mph: 5.0 seconds

60 to 0 braking: 127 feet

1/4-mile at MPH: 13.7 seconds at 102.7 mph

Production

Total Produced (Coupe Only): 5,808
 - Dark Highland Green: 4,377
 - Black: 1,431

It is interesting that, perhaps due to the relatively low sales numbers for the Blue Bullitt Edition model in 2001, Ford pared the color choices back down to two: the appropriate Dark Highland Green and black. The black Bullitt is a handsome car,

San Francisco is famous for its hill-staggered garages, and here the 2008 Bullitt Mustang really looks the part. Is it 1968 all over again?

Chad McQueen takes the Bullitt wheel of the 2008 Mustang Bullitt to try the car on for size in San Francisco. He clearly enjoyed the drive, prowling the same streets his famous father did four decades before.

A famously iconic Bullitt filming location is Larkin Street overlooking Alcatraz Island. The Mustang looks at home here, but it's also a spot in the film where the Charger famously bangs the wall and one of its many hubcaps is sent flying.

Back in Southern California, *Motor Trend* magazine road testing editor/driver Scott Mortara checks in with testing assistant and photographer Julia LaPalme prior to lining the 2008 Bullitt up for another assault on the quarter mile. Mortara said the car was "easy to launch down the drag strip and very consistent."

With *Motor Trend's* radar gun solidly locked on, the Bullitt chirps its tires down the quarter mile. In as much as Ford had yet to officially release this model, note the black tape over the rear gas cap badge to cover up the Bullitt lettering and logo for the drive home from San Francisco and around LA, as if no one saw this a new Mustang in Dark Highland Green and couldn't figure out what it was?

Ford snuck a pair of 2008 Bullitts up to San Francisco for its media, marketing, and PR photo shoots and issued this wonderful two-car image as a free downloadable computer desktop wallpaper or screensaver. Very shadowy and nicely done, although the movie chase scene didn't take place at night and seldom was the Mustang seen at night in the film but who cares. It's cool. (Photo Courtesy Ford Motor Company)

as the clean body and trim treatment suits itself well to this hue, but the tried-and-true Bullitt aficionados barked that it just isn't really a *Bullitt* Mustang unless it's Highland Green. Yet everyone happily agreed that the 2008/2009 bodystyle was much more similar to the 1968's look and profile and came off as a better tribute to the original than the 2001 model.

I was executive editor at *Motor Trend* magazine at the time this car was introduced, so to get some family perspective on the whole project, as well as to walk in the footsteps (and tire prints) of Bullitt himself, Chad McQueen joined us in San Francisco for our official road test of the new 2008 Bullitt. He had a somewhat-vested interest in driving this new Bullitt Edition, as he acquired serial number 001 of the 2008 production units. He also had serial 001 of the 2001 model, and this would round out a full complement of Bullitts. Chad was very pleased at the overall look and felt it captured the spirit of the original. He also liked the way the car handled and commented that it sounded good and offered ride quality and brakes that the 1968s could only dream of. He wanted to jump the car up and down Taylor Street, but we had to persuade him otherwise, since the car belonged to Ford, and we needed to get it back to *Motor Trend*'s performance test track in Los Angeles in one piece.

With the 50th anniversary of the original film coming for 2018, everyone wondered if there would be a third official Mustang Bullitt from Ford, as the Mustang platform, engine, and chassis architecture had been fully remodeled beginning with model year 2015. That question was resoundingly answered at the 2018 North American International Auto Show in Detroit. On that historic day, Ford rolled out a production-ready (for the 2019 model year) Mustang Bullitt edition car. This time, there was no teasing with a concept version like in 2000. The car was featured on the Detroit show stage alongside the long-thought-missing chassis 559 1968 hero/beauty car driven by Steve McQueen in the film. It proved the ultimate release party for this holy grail of Mustangs to be presented to the world in Detroit by Molly McQueen, Steve's oldest granddaughter, alongside the newest and arguably greatest Mustang Bullitt edition yet.

Molly McQueen, daughter of Steve's late daughter Terry, reveals the 2019 Mustang Bullitt to the assembled North American International Auto Show media crowd and the world in Detroit in January 2018. Molly and her cousin Madison are the third generation of McQueens that most resemble their famous grandfather. Naturally, it was an exciting moment, yet no one on hand expected what was coming within a few minutes of rolling the new car out on stage. (Photo Courtesy Ford Motor Company)

Talk about making a grand entrance. Much like a gladiator entering a Roman arena, Bullitt Mustang 559, driven by owner Sean Kiernan, enters Detroit's Cobo Hall for its big reveal at the North American International Auto Show in 2018. The assembled media and other attendees were simply shocked that the car was still in the hands of the family that owned it for more than three decades, that it was running and driving, and that it was blemished but so compellingly original. Camera shutters exploded at full speed, onlookers cheered, and owner Kiernan smiled and waved as he prepared to roll the original onto the stage to join the newest third-generation Mustang Bullitt along with Molly McQueen. Ford, Hagerty, the Historic Vehicle Register, Molly, and the Kiernans had created a genuine moment. Now it was confirmed that both of the movie Mustangs survived. Well done to everyone. (Photo Courtesy Ford Motor Company)

It was a big day at a big show for two big cars (metaphorically speaking). The long hiber-nating 559 1968 Bullitt Mustang hero/beauty movie car enjoys a grand reveal. Photos of this magic moment were uploaded to social media so quickly and in such quantity that Cobo Hall's internet servers overloaded and froze up several times. (Photo Courtesy Ford Motor Company)

Hey! Bill likes it! William Clay Ford II (executive chairman of Ford and a Mustang guy to the core) seems pretty happy to see the third-generation Mustang Bullitt in the Ford booth at the 2018 North American International Auto Show in Detroit. (Photo Courtesy Ford Motor Company)

2019 Ford Mustang Bullitt

This event rocked not only the assembled media and VIPs at the Detroit Auto Show preview but indeed the entire *Bullitt*sphere. Not only did Ford Motor Company celebrate the 50th anniversary of the making of *Bullitt* in the grandest of ways but it was also brilliantly punctuated by the fact that the 559 Mustang lived and existed in deeply original form. It was mechanically recommissioned to be a fully running and driving machine that looked and sounded exactly as it did banging gears through the streets of San Francisco in 1968 with Steve at the wheel. After so many years being considered missing in action, it remained in the quiet steward-ship of the Kiernan family. Sean Kiernan was on hand to celebrate the big event with Molly McQueen.

This newest Bullitt really has the goods to wear the name and the badge. It employs the Mustang Track Pack–equipped GT as a worthy starting point to become so far the ultimate Ford Bullitt tribute edition to date.

Handling
Standard
- 330-mm, 13-inch rear brake rotors with single-piston calipers
- Red-painted Brembo brake calipers
- Electronic line-lock (track use only)
- Independent rear suspension open
- Launch control (track use only)
- Selectable drive modes
- Selectable-effort electric power-assist steering (EPAS)
- Unique stability control, EPAS, and ABS tuning
- Monotube shocks, grippy bars, and rear cross-axis suspension joints
- Vented four-wheel disc brakes

Optional
- MagneRide damping system
- 3.73:1 Torsen limited-slip rear axle
- 5.0L Ti-VCT V-8 Open image overlay for 5.0L Ti-VCT V-8 rated at 480 hp

- Active valve performance exhaust system with quad tips
- Engine oil cooler
- 6-speed manual transmission with rev matching

Wheels and Tires
Standard
- 19-inch, five-spoke, bright-machined aluminum Heritage wheels with high-gloss black-painted pockets
- P255/40R19 front, P275/40R19 rear summer-only tires
- P255/40R19 front, 275/40R19 rear summer-only tires

Other Options
Standard
- Decklid spoiler delete
- Dual exhaust with quad tips with Nitro-Plate Black finish
- Easy Fuel capless fuel filler
- Daytime running lights
- LED fog lights
- LED headlights with LED signature lighting
- LED front park turn lamps
- Hood vents
- LED sequential taillights
- Mirrors (body-color, heated with integrated blind spot mirrors and turn-signal indicators)
- Pony projection lights
- Rear diffuser
- Bright beltline and window surround
- Faux gas cap on rear applique with Bullitt logo
- Unique front grille without pony badge
- Unique lower grille

Optional
- Blind spot information system (BLIS) with cross-traffic alert
- Aluminum foot pedals
- 12-inch LCD digital instrument cluster with MyColor
- Heated steering wheel
- Auto-dimming rearview mirror
- Autolights (automatic on/off headlights) with wiper activation

The 2019 Mustang Bullitt enjoys lots of appropriately blacked-out trim as did the movie cars. Ford displayed and photographed the new cars with movie-proper "JJZ 109" license plates to complete the effect. (Photo Courtesy Ford Motor Company)

When the movie Mustangs were modified for Bullitt duty in 1968, the original "dual dual" exhaust tips were cut off and tossed in the bin. This was not the case for the 2019 car. As said in that famous children's story, "All the better to hear you with," the third-generation Bullitt spoke deeply and loudly through quad exhaust pipes, which feature electrically actuated flapper valves that can be driver-selected to be either louder or quieter, depending upon mood, locale, and purpose. This is technology no one even dreamed of in 1968.

The 2019 Bullitt enjoyed every update and benefit given to the newest generation of Mustangs, including up-to-date and superb infotainment, plus a machined aluminum instrument panel, a Bullitt logo steering wheel Boss airbag, and a white shifter ball, as now worn by the 559 1968 Mustang. Plus, it had a superb leather-lined cabin, power everything, and the latest and greatest safety hardware—for jumping up and down the streets of San Francisco, of course.

Facing Page: When Ford introduced its newest Bullitt, it had not yet finalized the engine specs. At the time, it was quoted to have "at least" figures of 470 and 475 hp. It's always best to under-promise and over-deliver, and the final output number settled at 480. Ford's old FE 390 was a great engine back in its day but couldn't compete with what today's all-aluminum, four-cam, nearly 500-hp wonder can achieve in terms of performance, fuel mileage, and clean emissions.

Ford relied on expert perfor-mance and racing seat maker Recaro for the third-gen-eration Bullitt's new leath-er-wrapped sport seats. These seats are somewhat lighter than many production mod-els and offer superb support and substantial side-grip to hold you close during high-G cornering.

Ford reprised the strut tower brace with the Bullitt logo. Although, unlike the previous Ford Racing unit, this piece isn't engraved with the car's VIN. It looks great, sets the car apart from other Mustang models, and does the job in terms of sharper handling.

- Bright chrome door speaker surround
- Satin chrome instrument cluster register vents and cupholder surrounds
- Center console with full armrest
- Stitched center console lid, wrapped knee bolster with Dark Highland Green accent stitch and shifter boot
- Spindrift aluminum instrument cluster panel appliqué
- Center high-mounted dome lamp
- Cupholders
- Driver footrest
- Electronic locking center console
- Floor mats (carpeted, front)
- Illuminated glove box with lockable door and dedicated space for owner's manual
- Intelligent Access with push-button start
- Interior trunk release
- Leather-wrapped parking brake handle
- Leather-wrapped steering wheel with cruise and audio controls
- Tilt/telescoping steering column
- Map pockets (back of driver and front passenger seats; not available with optional Recaro seats)
- MyKey

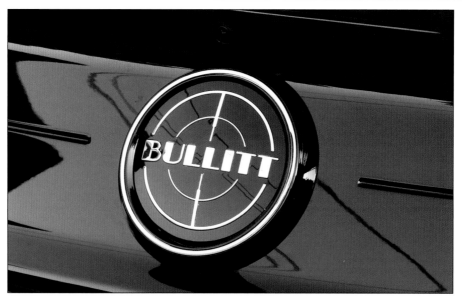

Another design element that Ford reprised for the third-generation Bullitt is the use of the faux gas cap as a way to display the Bullitt gunsight and logotype. Slick!

Part of Ford's deal to use the 559 Mustang to help create and introduce the third-generation Mustang Bullitt with the Kiernan family was that it spend time cross-pollinating its McQueen and film DNA from 1968 to 2019, which included visits to the Ford Design Studio, which was tasked with designing the new car. They looked great together, and this move obviously did the job. It also served to help educate younger studio staff members as to what Steve McQueen, the film, and the original cars were all about. Job well done. (Photo Courtesy Ford Motor Company)

- Windows (power; front one-touch up/down with Global Open)
- Powerpoints
- Premium door trim
- Soft door rollover
- Rearview camera
- Reverse sensing system
- Dual illuminated visor vanity mirrors
- Track Apps
- Universal garage door opener
- Bullitt aluminum door sills scuff plate
- Bullitt logo on driver airbag cover
- Unique white cue ball shift knob

The 2019/2020 Mustang Bullitt can be purchased in your choice of Dark Highland Green or Shadow Black, and as the car is currently offered for sale at the time of this writing, no production number or sales summary information are available.

This august gathering of Mustangs represents four generations and bodystyles of Bullitt-themed cars. From the left are the 2019, 1968, 2001, and 2008/2009 cars. They gathered at the Fabulous Fords Forever Car Show in Buena Park, California. It was the 2019 Bullitt's first showing on the West Coast.

STEVE McQUEEN EDITION

How to make an already very Steve McQueen Bullitt Mustang even a little more so? That was the driver behind the very limited production Steve McQueen Edition Bullitt Mustang model, which was the beautiful result of a like-minded joint venture between McQueen Racing, Steeda Performance, and Galpin Auto Sports. The employment and deployment of noted designer Freeman Thomas ensured that the look and cues would be just right. These design touches include a new set of special five-spoke alloy wheels that look "just right" and Steve McQueen signature badging in several places. There was a choice of naturally aspirated (at over 500 hp) or supercharged engine options. Only 300 cars will be built. (Photo Courtesy Steeda Performance)

In essence, all Ford-authorized and -built Bullitt Mustangs are Steve McQueen editions. Yet aftermarket high-performance purveyor Steeda Performance Vehicles, Ford, the McQueen family, McQueen Racing, and Galpin Motors have taken the concept a step further with an even more special edition with considerably amped-up performance that bears unique design features, further serialization, and Steve McQueen's signature.

The Steeda Steve McQueen Edition 2019 Bullitt Mustang began as a Ford production Mustang Bullitt in Dark Highland Green.

Steeda has been amping up Mustangs and a variety of hot Fords for decades. The company was first known for its high-performance suspension and exhaust systems but has expanded its portfolio of activities, including all

manner of components with limited-production runs of complete vehicle builds. One look at the 2019 Mustang Bullitt when it was announced by Ford convinced the Steeda folks they had to do something extra special with it. They approached the McQueen family through McQueen Racing (its business and licensing arm) about a limited-production run of a higher-performance, more exclusive Bullitt Mustang.

Steeda's media announcement neatly summarizes the program:

"McQueen Racing and Steeda, alongside Chad McQueen, have announced the launch of the official Steve McQueen Edition Bullitt Mustang in a limited production of only 300/year. Using the stunning new Ford Bullitt Mustang as a starting point, this ultra-high-performance edition has been purposely re-engineered to

One of the very first Steve McQueen Edition Ford Bullitt Mustangs visits Galpin Auto Sports (GAS) for a special television shoot. GAS president Beau Boeckmann (center, in all black) explains the Steeda car's special makeup equipment, design, and relationship to the GAS build team.

This is no mere Bullitt. The special faux gas cap badge incorporates Steve McQueen's autograph to inform everyone behind you that you're driving an extra-rare, unique, and fast limited-edition Bullitt Mustang. (Photo Courtesy Kirk Gerbracht)

This is the star of any car show: anywhere, any time. (Photo Courtesy Kirk Gerbracht)

This photo at the Galpin Auto Sports shop provides a good look at the unique 20-inch wheels designed by Freeman Thomas specifically for the Steeda Steve McQueen Edition Bullitt Mustang. The charcoal gray wheel finish is elegant and businesslike and pays modern homage to the 1968 movie cars.

deliver supreme performance, improved driving dynamics, and an increased exclusiveness for this iconic Mustang. The dedicated engineering and performance teams have spent considerable development time to create the most quintessential McQueen Mustang possible—The Steve McQueen Edition. The design spec was classic McQueen. Take an already excellent car and enhance power throughout the RPM band while improving the handling capabilities suitable for both the road and track and give the design an even more classically restrained but undeniably cool stance that is menacing yet understated.

"The substantial chassis, suspension, and drivetrain upgrades involved over 27 individual components that provided powerful and confident performance, and were all designed, engineered, and manufactured under strict ISO 9001:2008 certified standards in the U.S.A.

"'The Steve McQueen Edition Program Team had no limits in its quest to incorporate key components that strategically work cohesively together delivering maximum performance,' proclaimed Dario Orlando, president of Steeda. 'The entire Steeda team is proud

to bring our over 30 years of experience in designing, engineering, and manufacturing high-performance Mustang components to this exclusive developmental team.'

"In addition, with the dramatic power increases and changes to the suspension, it was necessary to also upgrade the wheel and tire fitment to give the car its distinctive stance. To accomplish this, the Steve McQueen Edition Project Team worked hand-in-hand with Chad McQueen and the team at McQueen Racing to design and engineer a modern reincarnation of the classic wheel that was on the original 1968 Mustang that Steve McQueen drove in the movie. After countless design iterations, a new Steve McQueen Edition aluminum wheel was conceived that provides a staggered wheel fitment and optimizes the Nitto NT555 G2 High Performance tires (275/35-20 front and 315/35-20 rear).

"'Ford's Mustang has always been a big part of my dad's legend,' Chad McQueen said. 'I wanted to kick the already-strong performance up several notches without losing that essential style that makes this car so desirable. Less is more. This Special Edition reflects the lessons my dad ingrained in me about what made his personal cars so desirable.'"

Standard Package Content

McQueen Racing Performance Suspension Upgrades by Steeda
• Front and rear sway bars with welded-in-place solid billet ends

• Billet aluminum front and rear sway bar mounts
• IRS subframe bushing support system
• IRS subframe alignment kit
• IRS subframe support brace
• Dual rate ultimate handling springs
• Bump steer kit
• Performance-tuned struts and shocks (not available with MagneRide suspension)

Steeda wasn't content to merely bolt on an off-the-shelf supercharger for its very special Steve McQueen machine, so each blower wears badging in green lettering to denote that it sits under the hood of a Steve McQueen Edition Bullitt Mustang. How much horsepower? How about 800.

- Performance wheel alignment
- Camber plates
- Ultra-Lite chassis jacking rails
- Extreme G-Trac K-member support brace
- Billet aluminum vertical links

McQueen Racing Powertrain Upgrades
- McQueen Racing performance tune (550 hp)
- Tri-Ax short-throw shifter
- Clutch spring assist with perch kit upgrade
- Black aluminum coolant tank
- Steve McQueen Edition wheels (20 x 10 inch front and 20 x 11 inch rear) with Steve McQueen Edition center caps
- Nitto NT555 G2 high performance tires (275/35-20 front and 315/35-20 rear)

McQueen Racing Interior Upgrades
- Steve McQueen Edition door sill plates
- Steve McQueen Edition dashboard serialization plate
- Steve McQueen Edition floor mats

McQueen Racing Exterior Upgrades
- Aerodynamic front fascia enhancement package
- Hood strut kit
- Engine compartment serialization plate
- Rear decklid emblem
- Car cover

Steve McQueen Edition Special Buyers Package
- Letter of vehicle authenticity
- Steve McQueen Edition key fobs
- Signed and numbered Steve McQueen Edition *Bullitt* archival print on fine art paper by Camilo Pardo
- Selection of exclusive Steve McQueen Edition apparel

Optional Equipment
- Steve McQueen Edition four-point roll cage (requires rear seat delete kit)
- Steve McQueen Edition six-point seat belts by Safecraft Safety Systems
- Steve McQueen Edition rear seat delete kit
- Steve McQueen Edition leather- and alcantara-wrapped steering wheel with green center stripe at 12 o'clock position (non-heated)
- Steve McQueen Edition Whipple Super-charger power upgrade (800 hp)
- Steve McQueen Edition Whipple Super-charger 10-rib pulley/belt upgrade
- McQueen Racing/Ford Performance severe duty IRS half-shaft upgrade (required with supercharger upgrade)
- McQueen Racing carbon fiber performance driveshaft assembly
  Note: Installation of this component may cause an increase in NVH (noise, vibration, and harshness)

Vehicle Orders, Reservations, and Sales
Steeda's media announcement continued, "The Steve McQueen Edition of the Bullitt Mustang is strictly limited to 300 serialized versions (globally) per year. Vehicle reservation deposits are being taken immediately from Steeda-certified Ford dealers and directly from retail customers."

The subtle yet effective design work was done by noted front line automotive designer Freeman Thomas (formerly of the VW, Audi, Porsche, and Ford Advanced Vehicle Design Studio). Particularly critical elements included the badges that incorporated Steve McQueen's signature, as well as a new 20-inch wheel design and finish more accurately inspired by the 15-inch American Racing Wheels Torq Thrust D rims run on the original movie cars.

Chad McQueen was particularly interested to ensure that any car with both the *Bullitt* name and his father's name was legitimate and performed at the very highest levels. He commented, "You won't believe how this car goes and handles. They not only got the look right but it's race car fast and will keep up with a surprising number of high-priced exotic sports cars."

Chapter 7

CELEBRATING BULLITT

A charming moment and scene from Bullitt, and a look into Steve McQueen's whimsical sense of humor, is when Lt. Bullitt stops at the market across the street from his apartment to buy a newspaper. After shuffling through his pockets a bit, he looks up to ensure no one might be watching and pounds on the top of the newspaper dispenser rack so it pops open without any payment. He then sheepishly steals a paper; the irony of course is that he's a police officer stealing a 25-cent newspaper. You can still visit this market, although the paper dispenser is long gone. If you look between McQueen's legs at about shin-level, you'll see portions of the Mustang parked in front of the blue Chevy and the white Austin-Healey on the street behind him. (Photo Courtesy ©/™ Warner Bros. Entertainment Inc. [sl9])

The 50th anniversary of the film has been celebrated in many ways and levels, officially and otherwise. The easiest way to mark five decades since the production of this movie is to watch it again. The San Francisco skyline has certainly evolved over time, yet many of the iconic locations and buildings captured in the film remain intact and recognizable. Not every spot is the same, but a considerable number of them are, so it's easy and fun to cruise around the city and visit them—as if to follow in Steve McQueen's larger-than-life footprints and tire tracks.

Inside the local market at 1199 Clay Street hangs this framed Steve McQueen/Bullitt photo montage. Even though the market isn't seen during the chase scene, it is located across the street from the building that was used as Lt. Bullitt's apartment building and is featured in a pair of scenes in the film.

LIFE & ARTS

Tuesday, October 9, 2018 | A13

CULTURAL COMMENTARY

High-Octane Cool

'Bullitt,' now 50, marked the height of Steve McQueen's action stardom

The film, directed by Peter Yates, still has wheels, thanks to its star's charisma and the snarling vigor of its car chase.

laconic as McQueen, without exuding quite the same charismatic appeal to young and old alike. Then came the generation of Arnold Schwarzenegger and Sylvester Stallone, each trumpeting the sex appeal of a muscular physique. Today actors like Tom Hardy and Dwayne Johnson seek to fill the shoes of a McQueen, who had suffered a brutal death from cancer at just 50 years of age.

You always felt that McQueen was the real deal, a rebel of flesh and blood with the carefree courage of an auto racer and the rumpled tenderness of a loner who had survived reform school and run away to join the merchant navy. "I'm not an actor, I'm a reactor," he told Yates during the filming of "Bullitt," and yet his early training at the Actors Studio nurtured some of his most beguiling traits—the defiant gaze that could change in an instant to a clown's split grin, or his habit of looking

It's still headline news. Five decades since it first appeared in theaters, Bullitt's 50th anniversary was celebrated in newspapers and magazines during the fall of 2018.

The cars clearly date the movie to 1968, and hair and clothing styles also pin the film to its time. Another indication of reference is that there's not a single cell phone or tablet reader to be seen. This rings loud and clear several times when Johnny Ross and Lt. Bullitt each ask a cabbie to pull over at the curb to hop out to a nearby phone booth, plunk in a stack of coins, and make a phone call. This is

In 2018, Bullitt mega enthusiasts Anthony Bologna, Frank A. Panacci, and the late Don Ciucci conspired to commission this great graphic to celebrate 50 years of Bullitt and further recognizes the greatest car chase ever filmed. This wonderful image smartly includes the Charger and the Mustang, which unfortunately too many Bullitt artworks do not. This was emblazoned on countless shirts and T-shirts produced and sold to benefit the Boys Republic school charity, to which Steve McQueen and the McQueen estate are deeply dedicated. (Photo Courtesy Anthony Bologna)

something you wouldn't see in real life these five decades on. The airport scenes are filled with PanAm Airlines Boeing 707 aircraft, none of which are in commercial use anywhere in the world these days. There's also a TWA jet in one scene, which is also a now-defunct air carrier brand. A very old style quip or fax machine is used by the police to print out photos. It used a screeching dial-up modem and rubber cups on which to place the handset to create the communication connection.

Previous Anniversary Celebrations

Bullitt turning 50 is by no means the first or only anniversary demarcation of the history of the film. The International Mustang Bullitt Owners Club (IMBOC) has often marked significant *Bullitt* anniversaries. One of the more recent took place just five years prior to this writing, when IMBOC members gathered in San Francisco to visit and drive many of the film's locations to commemorate the 45th

anniversary of the filming and release of *Bullitt*. San Francisco was literally awash in green Mustang tribute vehicles as well as black Dodge Chargers. Enthusiasts from not only around the United States but also from around the world participated in this celebration.

50th-Anniversary *Bullitt* Film Screenings

In 2018, the McQueen family, BCII Productions, and Warner Brothers conspired to film several minutes of additional content to be shown just prior to the film

Not every Bullitt anniversary celebration took place in San Francisco. Many of them needed little more than a big theater movie screening (remember this was before the advent of today's giant-screen digital TVs) because the film is so much more compelling up on a big screen and with theater quality sound. This postcard advertises a special 30th-anniversary screening of Bullitt hosted by the Jules Verne Foundation, honoring Steve McQueen with its "Legendaire" award, and Chad McQueen spoke at the showing. It was all a mere two decades ago.

A number of Bullittheads gathered in 2013 to commemorate Bullitt's 45th anniversary. This great photo from that event's film location drive in Guadalupe Canyon shows a handsome replica Charger (not purported as the missing movie Dodge) and a pair of Bullitt Mustang tribute machines. (Photo Courtesy Anthony Bologna)

The Friends of Steve McQueen Car and Motorcycle Show hosted an exclusive 50th-anniversary screening of Bullitt a few nights before the show in 2018.

That car show–sponsored screening was in a San Fernando Valley theater complex. Before the show, Neile Adams McQueen addressed the attendees about her memories and thoughts of Bullitt and the times in 1968 San Francisco.

Notice Galpin's special Steve McQueen Edition "JJZ 109" license plate. Not wishing to risk a ticket on the freeway, Galpin's Steve McCord brought the car to the screening inside an enclosed trailer.

Automotive royalty was in abundance at this screening, which included (from left) automotive artist Nicolas Hunziker (who creates the Steve McQueen Car Show program cover/poster art each year), automotive television's Wheeler Dealer Mike Brewer, Neile Adams McQueen (foreground in beige suit), surrounded by her 6-foot-5-inch grandson Chase McQueen, Madison McQueen, Monique Thomas, Renee Thomas, Galpin's Steve McCord, and designer Freeman Thomas.

Facing Page: The Mustang Owners Club of California was a joint sponsor of the 50th-anniversary screening, and its club members were out in force that night. The 1968 Bullitt tribute Mustang belongs to Dave Kunz, and the 2019 Mustang Bullitt was provided courtesy of nearby Galpin Motors.

at special 50th-anniversary screenings. It was my privilege to attend one of these events at a theater complex in the San Fernando Valley, and it was stirring to see Dave Kunz's outstanding 1968 *Bullitt* tribute Mustang alongside a new 2019 Ford Mustang Bullitt parked in front of the theater, and even more so to see *"Bullitt* Starring Steve McQueen" up on the marquee. There are several versions of the original film out in DVD release, and it's likely that more will follow.

Sheryl Crow CD Cover and Autographed Doorjam

Bullitt and Steve McQueen are just as much beloved in popular culture as they are in car or film culture. McQueen's name has been mentioned or recognized in an odd pop song here and there, but never more and never better than in Sheryl Crow's 2002 hit "Steve McQueen" with its driving beat, strong guitar melody and soulful vocals. The lines play perfect homage to the song's namesake, declaring that all she needs is a fast machine to make it out alive. Appropriately enough, the music video for this song includes Sheryl Crow at the wheel of a *Bullitt*-like Mustang being chased by a black Camaro (not a Charger), a Triumph motorcycle, and a Porsche, which were all McQueen trademark icons.

She was! The doorjamb of Dave Kunz's fine 1968 Bullitt *tribute Mustang wears this autograph. Kunz's car has been used by Ford for many show appearances and video shoots, so it's logical that this great-looking car and Sheryl Crow came in contact with each other at a* Bullitt- *or music-video-related shoot or event.*

Bullitt and *Fast N' Loud*

One of reality television's most popular automotive shows is *Fast N' Loud*, which features the Texas-based build shop Gas Monkey Garage and stars the handsome hot rodder Richard Rawlings and his merry band of car builders (nicknamed "the monkeys" after the garage). To kick off the show's 15th season on television in 2019 with something big, an idea developed among Rawlings and Chad, Madison, and Chase McQueen to build an authentic *Bullitt* tribute Mustang and take it to San Francisco and re-enact some of the more iconic passages of the chase scene.

The entire scenario—from Rawlings's first meeting with the McQueen family to the acquisition of a donor car to Chad

visiting the shop to evaluate the build and its progress to the trip to San Francisco—would all be filmed and edited together into a single two-hour episode season premiere of *Fast N' Loud*. Naturally, the car was built entirely on location at the Merrill, Texas-based Gas Monkey Garage. It was decided to focus only on building a Mustang for filming purposes. A current black Dodge Challenger stood in for the original Charger. The very special Steeda Steve McQueen Edition Mustang Bullitt was featured in some background and setup scenes.

The build was a tricky balancing act for the Gas Monkey team. Rawlings and Chad agreed and insisted on an authenticity-driven car that looked the part, could out-perform the original, and

Sheryl Crow's 2002 album C'mon, C'mon *remains one of her most popular. Perhaps it's because it features her smash hit "Steve McQueen."*

The Gas Monkey–built Bullitt tribute machine not only looks the part and talks the talk but it also walks the walk up and down the streets of San Francisco. (Photo Courtesy Anthony Bologna)

would survive three action-packed days of filming without a spare car to rely on in case of a mechanical breakdown or an accident. It had to be built beginning with a genuine 1968 Mustang fastback, as opposed to a new sheet metal recreation body shell that would be somewhat more fortified than the original movie cars. It also couldn't be built into a tube-framed tank that could withstand anything because that wouldn't look, drive, or feel like a real Mustang. The donor car was generally whole and sound, although it needed to be completely stripped for this resto-build. The build team somewhat spontaneously decided to seam-weld all of

Chief Gas Monkey Richard Rawlings watches the proceedings and helps direct the action from the seat of a 6.4-liter Hemi V-8-powered Dodge Challenger. Okay, it's not a Charger, but a black Mopar muscle car standing in for the Dodge was judged close enough for television. (Photo Courtesy Anthony Bologna)

Chad McQueen hops inside to size up the Gas Monkey Mustang for himself. He did some acting and race driving during his life and career, so the notion of staring into a TV camera wasn't foreign to him. (Photo Courtesy Anthony Bologna)

This shot of the Gas Monkey Mustang bouncing its way down Taylor Street provides a frame of reference for how steep these hills are and how out of control things could have gotten in 1968 or today, when creating and then recreating the famous chase scene. Drifter and stunt driver Chris Forsberg demonstrated remarkable car control and pulled off the jumps, burnouts, and turns with style and aplomb. (Photo Courtesy Anthony Bologna)

the body seams to add structural strength to the body/chassis without adding non-original structural tubing or other measures that were not appropriate to the feel and methods of 1968. For the remake, one car was used for the entire chase, which meant that the team had to be careful not to damage it. A skid plate and the reinforcement welding provided extra rigidity during the jumps.

Like the original car, Gas Monkey's Bullitt Mustang had a 390-ci big-block V-8 but sported better breathing 428 heads, a Holley Performance distributor, and dual quad carburation, which was something not found on the original movie cars. While the factory GT390 version had 325 hp and the film cars were amped up to perhaps 350, the new Gas Monkey Mustang had nearly double that amount of power, producing a claimed 600 hp. The factory 4-speed toploader manual transmission and front disc brakes remained the same, but an aluminum radiator was added to provide extra cooling capacity. A custom MagnaFlow exhaust system was also added to enhance the car's soundtrack. As the movie car's oil pan was blown apart at least once during the chase scene's continuum of hard landings, some additional protective structure was also built around the Gas Monkey Mustang's oil pan.

Unfortunately, neither Carey Loftin, Bud Ekins, nor Steve McQueen were around to drive for the *Fast N' Loud* chase scene recreation, so Rawlings and the crew decided to farm that job out to a working professional drift racing driver whom they felt was up to this challenging task. He chose Chris Forsberg, an experienced event and championship-winning drift racer. Drifters are known and recognized for their often incredible car control.

"I actually have no [wheel to wheel] racing experience and taught myself how to drive stick in my friend's Honda when I was 14 in my parents' backyard," Forsberg said. "From there, I eventually sold

"Hanging out with the bad guys' car. What would Lt. Frank Bullitt say, Ms. McQueen?" Madison McQueen frames up with Frank Panacci's spectacular replica of the 1968 Bullitt Charger. *She's very proud of her grandfather's legacy, and some of her artwork and clothing designs include his image and the livery of some of his more famous cars. (Photo Courtesy Anthony Bologna)*

"It's a wrap!" The Gas Monkey Garage build team and television production crew pulled off a successful visit to San Francisco and credibly traced the footprints of Bullitt *and recreated cars and moments from the movie's chase scene. Drift racer and stunt driver Chris Forsberg is in the foreground, giving a thumbs up. Just to the right of him is the show's star and prime mover Richard Rawlings, Chad McQueen is standing to the right of this shot in the blue Ford jacket and sunglasses, and he is flanked by his kids Madison (left) and Chase (right). The rest are hardworking mechanics and production crew. Everyone, including the cars, made it home safely from the risky stunts. It made a spectacular way for the* Fast N' Loud *show to begin a new season with this special two-hour episode. (Photo Courtesy Anthony Bologna)*

my truck and bought a Mazda RX7 when I was 17. I learned about drifting and was eager to become a better driver, so I taught myself how to control the car by watching car videos of drivers from Japan.

"In 2003, we started the first organized events on the East Coast, where I was able to hone my skills. I moved to California to enter into the first season of Formula Drift in 2004, where I finished on the podium and continue to compete to this very day, holding the records for the most championships, most podium finishes, and most head-to-head wins.

"My stunt driving background stemmed from my competitive side, as I was approached to take my sideways-driving skills to the production side of the world where more and more agencies wanted to see their cars sliding through corners."

Forsberg admitted being a big Steve McQueen fan and has seen *Bullitt* and many other McQueen films. He particularly commented on how "badass McQueen was for having performed so much of his own stunt work."

Naturally, it wouldn't be a modern

reality TV show without some drama to throw the proverbial wrench in the proceedings. The build constantly seemed behind schedule, which added to all of the tension that around the shop, especially during Chad McQueen's inspection/update visit. A test drive discovered a problem with the transmission, so a hasty disassembly and rebuild was in order. Then there was concern that recreating the famous reverse wheel-hopping smoky burnout with the new car at the intersection of Larkin and Chestnut Streets could damage either the transmission or the rear end. That was in addition to the natural pressure created by attempting to memorialize a three-week-long film shoot in the span of a three-day television re-enactment.

In the end, it turned out fine. The car, while not a perfect period clone of the movie stunt cars, was a beautiful build, looked the part, and performed well. It was more than credible for a television re-enactment plot. Forsberg drove well, and while not driving with quite the tail-out, tire-smoking style of McQueen and the original movie stunt driving team, the footage captured the car at speed and gave some better definition to how sharp the turns and steep the hills were. The Gas Monkey Mustang survived in one piece, seemingly no worse for wear. Of course, there was little concern for the condition and well-being of the black Dodge Challenger that stood in for the bad guys' Charger, so it put down massive, tire-melting, smoky burnouts one after another on demand.

Madison, Chase, and Chad McQueen were all on hand to watch the action. Steve McQueen's grandkids commented on tape how "crazy it is to be standing on this corner where Grandpa did these stunts 50 years ago." Chad admitted that he "got a little chill as the Mustang went by."

The production was a success. No one and no property were harmed, and the show was edited and aired to the pleasure of *Fast N' Loud* and *Bullitt* fans everywhere. And what became of the purpose-built

Mustang? As of this writing, it is being raffled off for charity. There's no question that Steve McQueen would have liked that.

Blue Bloods Television Episode Appearance

Tom Selleck's highly acclaimed television police drama series *Blue Bloods* dedicated its November 6, 2015, installment (season 6, episode 7) to *Bullitt* and more particularly to the on-screen theft of the famous *Bullitt* Mustang. Of course, at this point both of the original cars were still in hiding, so an accurate-looking clone was used as a handsome and appropriate stand-in. At one point, the detective played by actor Donnie Wahlberg calls it a "1968 Ford" and a police crime lab tech casually comments that "everyone's all in a tizzy over some used car" to imply that none of the younger *Blue Bloods* police force members know about *Bullitt* or Steve McQueen. However, Selleck's character puts them all in their place by reminding everyone, "It's what we call the good old days." When inspecting the car, post–theft recovery, Selleck looks the car over carefully and is clearly impressed. He can only utter a somewhat breathless "wow."

The car appears in several warehouse-style scenes and is seen only in static shots with no driving scenes or attempts to recreate any of the action from the film chase. It's a nice recognition for *Bullitt*'s original star and car.

1968 and 2019 Bullitts Star on *Jay Leno's Garage*

This amazing 2018 segment of *Jay Leno's Garage* was filmed at the Ford Proving Ground in Dearborn, Michigan. It opened with Jay at the wheel of a 2019 Mustang Bullitt. He cruised around the road course and looked in his rearview mirror, in an obvious and worthy homage to the scene in the film chase when the driver of the Charger saw Lt. Bullitt and the long-thought-lost 559 *Bullitt* Mustang in his rearview mirror. Owner Sean Kiernan was at the wheel, and when the two cars parked, Jay introduced himself to Sean and changed into an ill-fitting, several-sizes-too-small sport coat and blue turtleneck to mimic the outfit that Lt. Bullitt wore during the chase scene.

With a smile on his face and the lower portion of his stomach poking out a bit, Leno commented, "You know, Steve McQueen was all guts, and I'm all gut and no glory." Then, Leno took the wheel of the 1968 559 with Kiernan in the passenger seat and cruised around the Proving Ground for the cameras. He was clearly moved and impressed at the experience, having seen the film as a kid in 1968 and being dually impressed with McQueen and the car. Being one of the few people to have driven the car since its recommissioning, he dedicated the episode to the late Robert Kiernan and Sean Kiernan for being such worthy custodians of this significant piece of cinematic and automotive history.

Boys Republic School

Something you may not know about Steve McQueen is that he was practically an orphan and at best a troubled youth. It seems as if the Boys Republic School in Chino Hills, California, was made just for McQueen. His young single mother, after years of schlepping him around the country while trying to raise him, sent him to live with an uncle, which was also a less-than-successful endeavor in shaping him up. She ultimately brought him to this West Coast school for wayward kids, asked if they could help, and challenging the school to "see if it could make something of him."

The school, originally only for boys, was home to Steve for his senior year of high school. Its motto is "nothing without labor" and teaches teamwork, social skills, a variety of vocational skills, farming, animal husbandry, and culinary arts to at-risk children. In other words, for the privilege of room, board, support, education, and a fair shake at life, Boys Republic is a most-worthy spot for kids who have, for one reason or another, had a difficult childhood.

McQueen buckled down, worked hard, and successfully graduated from Boys Republic with a diploma before he enlisted in the military. He often credits the school for "saving his life" and financially supported the school for the rest of it. He often visited just to meet the kids, talk about their lives at school, shoot pool and play cards, and encouraged them always to "look out for each other" and to make something of themselves when they graduated.

It is to this end that the school holds the annual Friends of Steve McQueen Car and Motorcycle Show in his memory for his contributions and as a major fundraiser. Chad McQueen and philanthropic businessman Ron Harris serve as co-chairmen. The event began in 2008 in rather humble ways with about 75 or so cars and now has grown exponentially in size. It's a run-what-you-brung kind of event with a class or category for everything from rat rods to concours-quality hardware. There were more than 300 entries in 2019. Naturally, that included many Fords and Mustangs, with many of the latter painted Highland Green Metallic, including many 1968 Bullitt tribute clones, 2001 Bullitt-edition Mustangs, plenty of the 2008–2009 Mustang Bullitt GTs, plus a tantalizing roundup of new 2019s and a Galpin/Steeda McQueen Edition 2019 Ford Mustang Bullitt.

Each year's show is dedicated to one of McQueen's films, and *Bullitt* was recognized as the weekend's honored movie in 2012 and 2018 to commemorate *Bullitt*'s 50th anniversary. Each Friends of Steve McQueen Car and Motorcycle Show weekend includes a screening of the honored film at a nearby theater complex. Prior to the showing of the film in 2018, Neile Adams McQueen addressed the audience with thoughts and memories of the making of *Bullitt*, the cars, and the times.

Bullitt Wristwatch Helps Drive Toward a Cure

The 559 *Bullitt* Mustang owner Sean Kiernan and LA-area-based Public Relations Executive Deborah Pollack each lost a parent to Parkinson's disease. Pollack is also the executive director of Drive Toward a Cure, a nonprofit foundation that holds a variety of events and programs to bring awareness and raise funds for Parkinson's research. The two came together, along with artist Nicolas Hunziker (BRM watches) and the Grand National Roadster Show to create a special one-off chronograph wristwatch to commemorate *Bullitt*'s 50th Anniversary. This watch was raffled off, and all proceeds benefitted the charity and Parkinson's research.

Many things made this watch very special. BRM watches are rare and very expensive, the brand is a sponsor and supporter of the Boys Republic School's annual Friends of Steve McQueen Car and Motorcycle Show, and the dial was hand-painted by Hunziker. For Kiernan's contribution to the project, he donated a small chip of 559's original Highland Green Metallic paint that was encased inside the watch. The watch was initially valued at $30,000, but it reached much further out in the charity-sphere and raised (between ticket sales and matching donations) more than $50,000 for Parkinson's research.

(Photos Courtesy drivetowardacure.org)

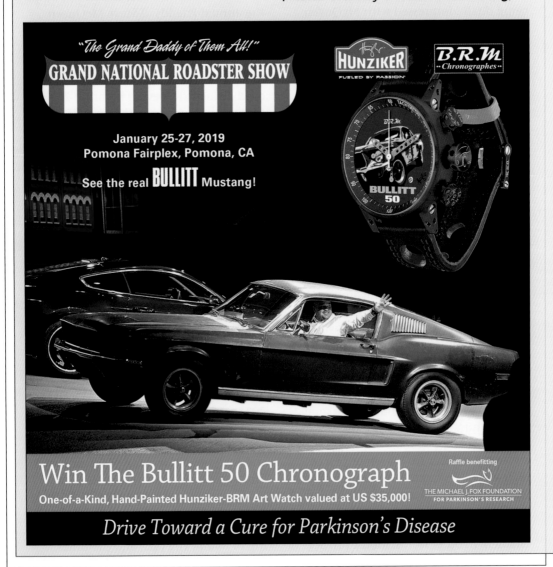

"The Grand Daddy of Them All!"

GRAND NATIONAL ROADSTER SHOW

HUNZIKER
FUELED BY PASSION

B.R.M
-Chronographes-

January 25-27, 2019
Pomona Fairplex, Pomona, CA

See the real **BULLITT** Mustang!

BULLITT 50

Win The Bullitt 50 Chronograph

One-of-a-Kind, Hand-Painted Hunziker-BRM Art Watch valued at US $35,000!

Raffle benefitting

THE MICHAEL J. FOX FOUNDATION
FOR PARKINSON'S RESEARCH

Drive Toward a Cure for Parkinson's Disease

The baseball team at Boy's Republic. Steve's in the back row, fourth from right.

These wonderful archival photos show various stages of Steve McQueen's life at Boys Republic. He was there for some part of what would have ostensibly been his junior and senior years in high school. He successfully graduated from the school before he enlisted in the military. You'll spot him in the baseball team photo (wearing a hat) in the back row fourth from right. Looking every bit the successful actor and movie star he was, here the now-adult Steve McQueen visits the school to talk to the kids, shares his story, and listens to their stories and dreams. It is amazing how many of these kids, who (when younger) were street criminals or had washed out of the foster care system and have gone on to become contributing adults with great families, careers, and success stories of their own. The bronze plaque memorializes his time at the school and philanthropic support of the students and the school. (Photo Courtesy Boys Republic)

The plaque reads:

STEVE McQUEEN RECREATION CENTER
STEVE McQUEEN
1930 TO 1980
HE CAME HERE AS A TROUBLED BOY, BUT LEFT HERE
AS A MAN. HE WENT ON TO ACHIEVE STARDOM IN
MOTION PICTURES, BUT RETURNED TO THIS CAMPUS
OFTEN TO SHARE OF HIMSELF AND HIS FORTUNE.
HIS LEGACY IS HOPE AND INSPIRATION TO THOSE
STUDENTS HERE NOW AND THOSE YET TO COME.
RENOVATION AND ADDITION COMPLETED NOVEMBER 1982

The Boys Republic monument reads:

BR
FOUNDED 1907

SELF GOVERNANCE
"Youth thrive on responsibility.

With guidance they will govern themselves and become responsible contributing members of society."
Max Scott

CITIZENSHIP OATH
I do solemnly swear

That as a citizen of Boys Republic,

I will observe the laws,

I will respect the rights and property of others,

I will recognize appointed authority,

And that I will contribute to this community in whatever ways I can.

NOTHING WITHOUT LABOR

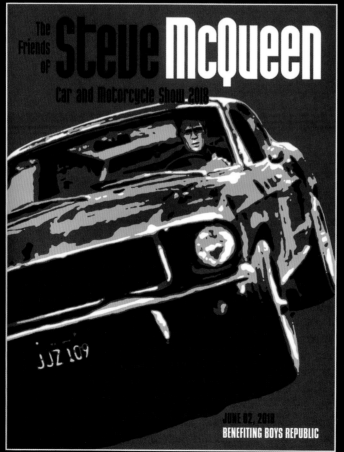

One of the alumni buildings on the Boys Republic campus offers this exhibit to honor the life of its most highly visible and best-known alums.

The Friends of Steve McQueen Car and Motorcycle Show has twice been built around and dedicated to Bullitt. The most recent was in 2018 to celebrate the famous film's 50th anniversary. This memorable program cover and poster was painted by McQueen family friend, noted artist, and racer Nicolas Hunziker.

Bullitt club members from around the world made the pilgrimage to Boys Republic in Chino Hills, California, to celebrate Bullitt 50 with the school, family, and other like-minded enthusiasts. It was a spectacular show that year that included lots of Highland Green Metallic Mustangs, a pre-event Bullitt screening, and a gala fundraiser. (Photo Courtesy Kirk Gerbracht)

Check out this near perfectly choreographed lineup of 2001 Mustang Bullitts from the 2018 Friends of Steve McQueen Car and Motorcycle Show. (Photo Courtesy Kirk Gerbracht)

Besides all of the 2001, 2008/2009, and 2019 Ford Mustang Bullitt edition cars on hand at the 2018 Boys Republic show, it's only logical that the original 1968 movies cars would be represented. They were by several handsome examples. (Photo Courtesy Kirk Gerbracht)

Now that's clever. A Bullitt art piece made up of, well, bullets. (Photo Courtesy Kirk Gerbracht)

This impressive lineup of Nicolas Hunziker show program and poster art gives an idea of some of the great Steve McQueen films that have been recognized and honored by the Boys Republic event weekend over recent years. (Photo Courtesy Kirk Gerbracht)

With the introduction of each new generation of official Ford Mustang Bullitt models, Chad McQueen works with Ford to reserve serial number one for his own collection. In the case of the 2019 Mustang Bullitt, he decided to put the car up for sale at the Barrett-Jackson Collector Car Auction in Scottsdale, Arizona, as a 100-percent charity lot with all proceeds benefitting Boys Republic. Here's the car on the block under the Barrett-Jackson Big Top, which is no longer actually a tent but now a permanent building, although the nickname has stuck. Tens of thousands of attendees, and hundreds of thousands more virtually witnessed the first third-generation Bullitt go under the gavel at no reserve, which means there was no minimum bid or guarantee and that the car would sell to the highest bidder. Barrett-Jackson takes no commissions on these charity lots, which means that all of the proceeds would go directly to Boys Republic. (Barrett-Jackson Photo, Courtesy Ford Motor Company)

The bidding for 2019 Mustang Bullitt serial number one was somewhat fast and furious. The gavel fell on a high bid of $300,000, which was a considerable donation over and above a new car with a sticker price of just over $50,000. Up on the auctioneer's stage, just above the block, you can see Chad McQueen with his arms up in the air. He is standing between Barrett-Jackson Chairman Craig Jackson (left) and company President Steve Davis, who also have their arms raised in celebration of this landmark auction event and important donation. (Barrett-Jackson Photo, Courtesy Ford Motor Company)

In 2018, a deeply enthusiastic group of Mustangers and Bullittheads created the "2018 HoonDog Legend Lives Route 66 Tour" as an homage to the Mother Road and a fun and innovative way to road trip with the group from Chicago to Chino Hills for the Boys Republic Friends of Steve McQueen Car and Motorcycle Show. They pulled it off with support from Ford Motor Company, Team Mustang, Ford Performance, and the HoonDog Performance Group (HPG). Ford pitched in a 2019 Mustang Bullitt prototype just to make the drive that much more interesting, and everyone who drove out entered their car in the show, which further added to the Field of (Highland Green Metallic) Dreams in Chino Hills that year. (Photo Courtesy Cole Quinnell, HoonDog Performance Group)

Bullitt Mustang tributes and clones of all ages participated in the HoonDog drive. There was no requirement that every participant's car be a Mustang or a Bullitt edition car, but most of them were. Needless to say, the group stopped traffic in every small town they visited or cruised through on their way west. (Photo Courtesy Cole Quinnell, HoonDog Performance Group)

Bullitt Mustang Tributes and Clones

Since the actual movie cars were missing in action for so long, many enterprising and devout Bullitt enthusiasts elected to build their own versions of the movie cars. This can and has been done at many levels. For some car owners, a Highland Green Metallic Mustang or an all-black Charger paint job will suffice. Yet to impress the *Bullitt* faithful, it takes more than paint. Serious *Bullitt*eers like Glen Kalmack, Frank A. Panacci, and Dave Kunz have gone extra miles to make sure their movie car tributes are as accurate of *Bullitt* tribute machines as is reasonably possible. See Appendix A for Kalmack's catalog of changes and mods that were done to the original Mustangs to make them movie stars, and even though some of these upgrades take a bit of work and parts hunting to pull off with absolute accuracy and authority, it's as accurate of a to-do list as anyone has ever assembled.

When contemplating his own Bullitt *movie tribute car, San Francisco Bullitthead Frank A. Panacci couldn't decide between the Mustang and the Charger, so he built one of each. They couldn't look any more at home than in the city with swirling fog and the Golden Gate Bridge in the background. (Photo Courtesy Anthony Bologna)*

Facing Page: This great snapshot would make you think the whole group was made of up 2008/2009 Mustang Bullitts, but that's not the case. There were 1968s, 2001s, and a much-welcomed 2019 along for the ride, plus a passel of other Mustangs of all stripe and color. You can just about hear Willie Nelson singing "On the Road Again," or the cymbals, piano, and brass of the jazzy Bullitt *movie score. (Photo Courtesy Cole Quinnell, HoonDog Performance Group)*

Panacci's Mustang has appeared in video and TV shoots, as it is being rigged up here. That's Frank at the wheel. (Photo Courtesy Anthony Bologna)

Frank A. Panacci's Bullitt Charger tribute car is widely regarded as one of the most authentic extant, and you can see why. The look, stance, and every detail is period correct. The year 1968 was an all-new bodystyle for Charger, and it remains among collectors' favorites. (Photo Courtesy Anthony Bologna)

All the badging and emblem trim on Panacci's Charger is as fresh as 1968, as is the proper matching black vinyl top. The car wouldn't be right without this detail.

Given that one of the movie Chargers was a 4-speed and the other a console-shifted automatic, Panacci was correct and wise in leaving his as-built-automatic transmission car in this form.

The only major detail about the engine compartment in Frank Panacci's Charger that isn't period original is the finned aluminum MoPar Performance valve covers. Otherwise, it's all 440 and looks and runs great.

Of course, this car wears the proper and correct hubcaps. I wonder if any of them went missing like the Chargers used in the movie that seemed so intent on scattering them around San Francisco during the chase scene?

The Panacci Charger even goes so far as to carry a replica movie-correct California license plate. Note the Friends of Steve McQueen Car Show license frame.

This is a proper healthy 390, which is the same engine that Kunz's car and the movie Mustangs had. The primary difference here is that Kunz's car is equipped with factory air-conditioning, as you can see from the large compressor mounted at the right front of the engine, which the movie Mustangs didn't have. (Photo Courtesy Ford Motor Company)

Dave Kunz's fabulous S-Code GT390 Bullitt tribute Mustang has been used many times by Ford at shows and for various photo shoots and events, but it was never better than for the media launch program in San Francisco for the 2001 Mustang Bullitt. The more things change, the more they stay the same. (Photo Courtesy Ford Motor Company)

Of the many Bullitt Mustang replicas, tributes, and clones built over the years, few have gotten it more right than deeply committed Bullitt enthusiast Glen Kalmack. Every touch and detail is just right. It was no small effort to curate, assemble, or recreate all the bits and bobs needed to make his car as close to the movie cars as reasonably possible. (Photo Courtesy Glen Kalmack Collection)

This is no replica. It is one of the original plates used on the actual movie cars. Kalmack went through considerable effort and expense to acquire this plate and certify it to be the actual period piece. Note the chipped paint; it all just completes the look and correctness Kalmack was after. (Photo Courtesy Glen Kalmack Collection)

Facing Page: Kunz's Mustang is parked on Larkin Street, overlooking Alcatraz Island. Unlike the Charger, not a single hubcap was lost in the making of this photo.

Something many Bullitt Mustang recreators don't often bother with is the effort to recreate the underbody camera mounts used on the movie cars. As you can see, the construction and materials are relatively straightforward and the cost is minimal, but they add another layer of realistic effect to any Bullitt tribute Mustang. (Photo Courtesy Glen Kalmack Collection)

The visual effect the recreated camera mount brackets have on the finished car are subtle but effective. It's something any committed Bullitt enthusiast will look for and recognize. (Photo Courtesy Glen Kalmack Collection)

As further evidence of the effort Glen Kalmack went to properly recreate the movie cars, check out this three-button switch mounted to the turn signal stalk. Contrary to some opinion, this was not installed to control the cameras but only to flash brightly in case a turn signal was accidently flipped on. As you can imagine, a flashing turn signal during the chase scene would have been incongruous. (Photo Courtesy Glen Kalmack Collection)

THE ENDURING LEGACY OF BULLITT AND STEVE MCQUEEN

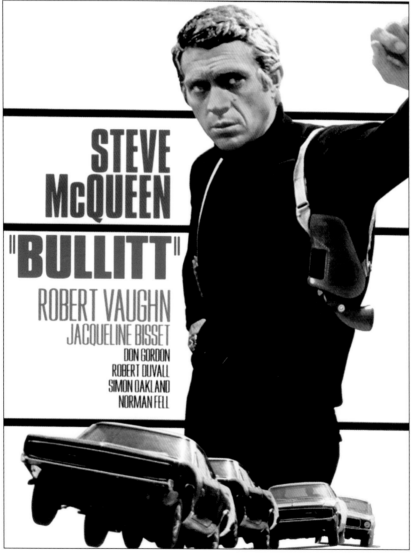

The pulse-pounding car chase was such an important element of Bullitt that it's even referenced at the bottom of the movie's official poster, which oddly enough shows multiple Chargers and only one Mustang. This iconic image of McQueen as Lt. Frank Bullitt made it abundantly clear who is the picture's star. This image was also used on countless theater lobby cards and 8 x 10 glossy PR still photos. (Photo Courtesy ©/™ Warner Bros. Entertainment Inc. [sl9])

Ford more than celebrated Bullitt's 50th anniversary and the launch of the third-generation Mustang Bullitt by helping bring the long-thought-lost 559 Mustang back into the public's eye at the 2018 Detroit Auto Show. Here, the hero/beauty 1968 and the new 2019 line up for a photo at Ford's Michigan Proving Grounds. (Photo Courtesy Ford Motor Company)

This charming movie premiere night photograph captures the look of 1968 perfectly. Unfortunately, we don't know the location of this singular standalone Tivoli Theater, but it's our estimation, based on the Spanish-language signage, that this street scene took place in a Spanish-language European country or in South America. No matter, the way these theatergoers are dressed and the cars parked on the street, the signage and decorations are pure late 1960s. A marvelous moment in time. (Photo Courtesy ©/™ Warner Bros. Entertainment Inc. [sl9])

Bullitt was released into national theater distribution on October 17, 1968, and grossed more than $40 million on its initial $4 million production budget. The film was ultimately released internationally, and while it was a clear box-office smash in North America, it also drew substantial viewership around the world, primarily in places where Steve McQueen was already a popular star, such as France, the UK, and Japan. *Bullitt* earned two Academy Award nominations for Best Sound and Best Film Editing, and it won the latter. *Bullitt* has been released and re-released on VHS, DVD, and Blu-ray formats several times, and at least once in a two-disc special edition set with one disc containing the film and a second filled with special features, including biographical information on several of the actors, director's commentary by Peter Yates, the theatrical trailer, and many minutes of commentary and interview material with Steve McQueen. There's also a brief but excellent video online called *The Making of* Bullitt that includes action footage of Bill Hickman and Steve McQueen practicing high-speed, door-to-door driving to prepare for the filming of the chase scene.

Toy stores, hobby shops, model shops, eBay, and the internet are chock-full of a wide variety of Bullitt *collectibles, many of which are officially licensed by the McQueen family and estate. Far too many are not, so shop carefully. You can find Hot Wheels-sized models of the* Bullitt *Chargers and Mustangs, often in sets, in addition to tiny McQueen action figures to complete your* Bullitt *library or bookcase collection. The specially labeled bottle of wine in the top center of this photo was bottled for the Friends of Steve McQueen Car and Motorcycle Show in 2018, and featured that year's Nicholas Hunziker painting that highlighted McQueen at the wheel of the* Bullitt *Mustang. (Photo Courtesy Mel Stone)*

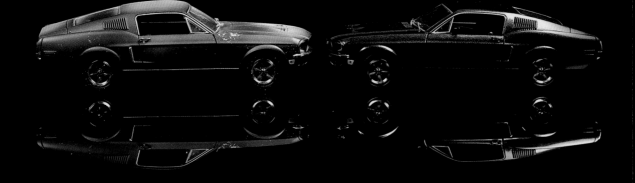

Most of the diecast models and toys depicting the Bullitt Mustang invariably show it with shiny green paint, which is understandable. Once the 559 Mustang was back in the public eye, model makers came out with a new edition that showed the car in its current, fully patinated condition. You can decide which you like best, but this meant that enthusiasts didn't need to buy a shiny model then convert it to barn-find condition with cleanser and other ageing methods. (Photo Courtesy Mel Stone)

For those who wish to collect *Bullitt* memorabilia, there is a wide variety of diecast models of the Mustang and Charger, and some of them officially licensed by the McQueen estate but some are not. There are also dolls and figurines in the marketplace; eBay is full of it. Every once in a while you'll find a reproduced copy of the *Bullitt* script or screenplay, which is also good fun reading and will tell you a lot about the plot and various scenes and lines in the film.

The Persol sunglasses made so famous by McQueen in *Bullitt* and other films have been reproduced and licensed by Persol. They are currently available under model number 714. The watch that McQueen wore in *Bullitt* on his right wrist even though he was right-handed is a Benrus Series 3061. It's a solid, reliable, civilian version of a military-style watch. This watch has not been reproduced or reissued but is relatively available and affordable through estate and special-interest vintage watch sources.

Should you wish to have a new, authentic, officially licensed watch just like Steve wore, look no further than TAG Heuer, which has updated and reproduced the iconic square-cased Monaco self-winding chronograph that Steve McQueen so famously wore as American racing driver Michael Delaney in his epic endurance racing drama *Le Mans* in 1971. It is available with the same blue dial as seen in the film, a limited-production Steve McQueen edition, plus others with black and Gulf blue and orange dials.

Joe Faccenda remembered, "I was working at a gas station on Filbert and Columbus and I noticed a camera crew on the building across the street pointing a camera up Filbert Street. There weren't any police blocking off streets or stopping traffic. Knowing that there was a movie being filmed in town with Steve McQueen, I got curious and walked to Filbert Street to see what was going on. As I got there, I saw the black Charger go by, and when I did go into the street, the green Mustang with

There will never be another Steve McQueen or Frank Bullitt, but you can share a bit of that famous style by wearing today's modern edition of their Italian shades. Eyewear maker Persol, which loosely translates to "for sun," reissued McQueen's now-iconic folding sunglasses frames some years ago. McQueen always seemed to be wearing those sunglasses in tortoiseshell frames, although they are also offered in black and a somewhat-clear plastic in a few different sizes. Initially, there was a limited-production Steve McQueen edition released. The model number is 714 and you can find them at most fashion eyewear stores, directly from Persol, and a variety of sources online. There are several unscrupulous outfits producing knockoffs, so shop carefully to make sure you're getting authentic Persols and thus the real McQueen.

An original Heuer Monaco of 1969/1970 as worn by Steve McQueen as American racing driver Michael Delaney in Le Mans. This piece was highly innovative in that it was the very first commercially produced self-winding chronograph watch, and its square case design made it utterly unique. Today's TAG Heuer company has updated and reintroduced this classic model in this exact blue main dial color and in a variety of other looks: black main dial, Gulf Blue and Orange, etc. What is most unique about this original case design is that while the stopwatch function "pusher" buttons are located on the right side of the watch, the winding main stem is located on the left side of the case. This is because, at the time, Heuer had difficulty packaging the winding stem, the pusher buttons, and the self-winding mechanism all on the right side of the watch. Today's modern Monacos have since moved the winder to the more expected right-hand side of the case. (Photo Courtesy McQueen Racing)

Just two years after the making of Bullitt, Steve McQueen was hard at work on his endurance racing magnum opus film Le Mans released in 1971. McQueen was again the defacto director and stunt coordinator and did a considerable amount of his own high-speed driving in the film. (Photo Courtesy McQueen Racing)

You can bet that detailed aspects of the chase scene were being planned at this moment with director Peter Yates (left), car builder and camera car driver Max Balchowsky (back to camera), McQueen (making the hand gestures), and stunt coordinator/drive Carey Loftin (right). Note the interested onlookers in the background. Among them is young Joe Faccenda (standing, back row, far right, in leather jacket, right hand in pocket). He stumbled, literally and figuratively, onto the set. See epilogue for his remembrances. (Photo Courtesy ©/™ Warner Bros. Entertainment Inc. [sl9])

Steve McQueen behind the wheel had to go around me.

"A couple of minutes later, a guy that looked upset walked toward me with a walkie-talkie and told me that I 'f——ed up the take.' They had sent him down to make sure I didn't do it again. I told him that I was working at the gas station and needed to move cars around so I could change the oil on one of them. He let me go on with my business and then I moved my grey Chevelle SS to the first parking spot on the sidewalk on Filbert Street. After I did that, I saw the Charger and the Mustang coming toward me again. At that point, the guy they had sent to watch me so I didn't mess up any more takes started yelling at me and told me to get back over to where he was standing. I started walk-ing toward him slowly and stopped to lean on a car. He wasn't very happy about that, but they didn't want to have to do another take. If you look quickly in that scene, you can see me and my Chevelle.

"That's the only picture I have of that car. I also witnessed two other scenes. I was standing behind the camera man when they shot the scene where he missed the turn and burned rubber in reverse. I was also at the bottom of the Taylor Street hills when the cars were flying down and made the turn to go up Filbert Street.

"Between takes, Steve McQueen would put on a show for us doing wheelies up Taylor Street on his Triumph motorcycle."

All said and done, how does one sum up the greatest car chase scene ever filmed, by one of the most-iconic Hollywood

We know that Steve McQueen always had at least one motorcycle with him on any given set, and this big Triumph was on set in San Francisco. Among the many things young Joe Faccenda recalls from his somewhat accidental visit to a couple of the Bullitt chase scene filming locations was watching McQueen ride wheelies up the hilly streets of the city. Besides the visuals offered by these streets, McQueen realized, while spending time riding around with costar and pal Don Gordon, that the geography of San Francisco could serve well for the raucous car chase scene he envisioned for Bullitt. (Photo Courtesy ©/™ Warner Bros. Entertainment Inc. [sl9])

It's good fun to thumb through period Bullitt memorabilia, such as this handsome production/PR still of Steve at the wheel of the Mustang, looking his very Lt. Bullitt best. Note the imprint at the lower right that proclaims "dans une production SOLAR," which is in French and indicates the film was a SOLAR Production. (Photo Courtesy ©/™ Warner Bros. Entertainment Inc. [sl9])

actors of all time, in what is certainly among his most popular films? In a 1968 *Motor Trend* magazine interview, McQueen said, "I always felt a motor racing sequence in the street, a chase in the street, could be very exciting because you have the reality objects to work with, like bouncing off a parked car. An audience digs sitting there, watching somebody do something that I'm sure almost all of them would like to do."

No kidding, Steve.

The star of Steve McQueen (1930–1980) is shown on the Hollywood Walk of Fame.

Stop the Press!
The 559 *Bullitt* Mustang Sells at Auction for $3.71 million!

Mecum's auction and security staff created a moving cordon in order to escort the Mustang up the block. Every cell phone camera in the house was certainly rolling in the hopes of catching this magic auction moment. (Photo Courtesy Anthony Bologna)

It was no small effort to get the car from display to the Mecum auction block, but it happened without fault. As you'd expect, the opening bid of $3,500 immediately jumped into the millions of dollars. The bidding was, to riff off of the movies of the same name, fast and furious. (David Newhardt Photo, Courtesy Mecum Auctions)

This amazing bird's-eye photo gives an idea of the size of the room where the 559 Mustang had yet another 15 minutes of fame. If you look in the middle of this sea of auction house humanity, you'll spot the Mustang's green roof, which is the only part of the car visible beyond the crowd. (Photo Courtesy Mecum Auctions)

When Hagerty Insurance Company brought the 559 Bullitt Mustang to the 2018 Amelia Island Concours d'Elegance, the company, who insures this one-of-a-kind automotive treasure, pulled out all the stops in building a special marquee and display for the seldom-seen Mustang. Most onlookers, obviously seeing the car for the first time, were surprised (some most pleasantly, a few others not) at what worn, original, and highly patinated condition the car was in. Those who appreciate originality and preservation felt the car looked perfect as presented, while others felt that such a rare and prized bit of movie, pop culture, and automotive history should be in immaculate condition, sans rust, scrapes, dents, and faded paint. I disagree as this way the car has all of its hard-earned stories intact. Most of them were earned in San Francisco in 1968, because a car can only be original once.

Following the mechanical recommissioning of the 559 *Bullitt* Mustang, and its subsequent debut at the 2018 North American International Auto Show in Detroit, the Kiernan family took their famous movie car on what ostensibly turned out to be a near two-year victory tour.

The car was also displayed at the Geneva International Auto Salon in Switzerland, the Amelia Island Concours d'Elegance, and made an "up the driveway" road course at the Goodwood Festival of Speed in England. It also visited San Francisco for appearances and photo and video shoots. It was written about and featured in countless magazine articles and video

The 559 earned a special preservation award that day at Amelia Island, and owner Sean Kiernan drove the car up to the podium to collect the trophy. The engine sounded sharp and crisp, and the exhaust pipes barked appropriately.

Ford brought the 559 and a new 2019 Mustang Bullitt to the Goodwood Festival of Speed in England to help introduce the new car in the UK. Steve McQueen and Bullitt are very popular in Europe, so the international crowd cheered the pair. There was also a black Charger on hand, so the Mustang and the Charger took a separate lap together sans the new car. (Photo Courtesy Ford Motor Company)

The Bullitt Mustangs, 1968 and 2019, really wowed the crowd at the Goodwood Festival of Speed in England. The differences and similarities between the two cars, born five decades apart, are too numerous to count. One thing that particularly strikes us is the evolution in wheel and tire design and sizes. The original wears aftermarket 15-inchers, about the largest you'd find on a street car at the time, and relatively tall sidewall 70 series bias ply tires. The new car has modern-sized wheels with low-profile performance rubber that only a race car in 1968 could even hope for. No matter, the cars are clearly related, and the assembled onlookers obviously didn't want to miss the action. Note that not a single spectator is sitting down in the grandstands. (Photo Courtesy Ford Motor Company)

The 559 "returns to the scene of the crime" and visits San Francisco for photo and video shoots and a local car show. If it weren't for all of the modern cars in the foreground and background of this wonderful photo, you wouldn't be wrong to think it was 1968 all over again. (Photo Courtesy Anthony Bologna)

Today 559's engine compartment is clean stock and tidy, yet it is hardly over-fluffed or overtly concours. This open-element Ford Hi-Po air cleaner certainly isn't the factory stock piece and was added either by the Balchowskys or as a replacement when the original reputedly went missing along the trail. The chromed valve covers are absolutely stock and proper for the GT390 4V engine option. The channel-shaped stamped shock tower braces are natural water and rust catchers, and Sean Kiernan wisely chose not to replace or repaint them during the recommissioning. The tops of the shock towers clearly show the red-painted Koni high-performance shocks installed in 1968 for movie car duty. (Photo Courtesy Ford Motor Company)

Today 559's interior is worn but not tatty, and in generally clean and original condition. Somewhere along the ownership trail, the stock Ford shifter was binned in favor of this Hurst shifter that wears a white shifter ball. The car didn't have this shifter configuration during filming in 1968. (Photo Courtesy Anthony Bologna)

shoots. The world was truly informed and celebrated that the original hero/beauty *Bullitt* Mustang lived.

Many were taken aback when in August 2019, Mecum Auction Company announced that the thought-lost-but-now-found *Bullitt* Mustang 559 hero/beauty car that belonged to the Kiernan family had been consigned for auction sale at the company's Kissimmee, Florida, collector car auction scheduled for January 2020.

Of course, the *Bullitt* and collector car communities were abuzz with, "Why are they selling it?" and "What'll it sell for?" The former is more easily quantifiable. Being the custodian of such a significant piece of Steve McQueen, film, and pop culture history isn't an easy thing and is something Sean Kiernan and his family had grappled with since the mid-1970s. Once he and his late father Robert had decided in 2000 to get the car back in shape mechanically and share it with the world. Sean has since done everything with it he could possibly wish to accomplish. It had been a star player in concert with Ford, appearing at two major international auto shows to help premiere new Bullitt edition Mustangs. It wowed the

crowd at the Goodwood Festival of Speed and appeared at countless other significant events. The 559 was documented and memorialized in the Library of Congress and the HVA Historic Vehicle registry. The Kiernan family's life had evolved—Sean was married, divorced, married again, and is now a father, so the time had come.

Mecum committed considerable resources to promote the car to an international audience and took it to each of its remaining collector car sales during the latter portion of 2019. It was on display in a special glass garage and appeared on television many times. Interesting yet completely transparent was the fact that the car was offered in the auction sale at "no reserve," which meant that the highest bid, be it a hundred dollars or a billion, would buy the car. The car was truly for sale and wasn't required to hit any artificially established minimum floor to be sold. Kiernan was clear and commented in numerous interviews that he "didn't want to have to sell it twice, and this was the right way to close the book on the car in his family's lives."

He didn't need to be worried about interest or demand. Kissimmee is Mecum's largest and most-highly attended sale on

The Mecum Auction company wanted people to be able to see the 559 Bullitt Mustang clearly and from all angles but eschewed the constrictive look of ropes and stanchions in favor of this portable glass garage that gave everyone a view from all angles while protecting the car from damage or anyone breaking off or stealing a souvenir bit or piece of the car. It made for a dramatic presentation wherever the car went on the Mecum Auction calendar and was displayed. Hearing the engine fire up in this small, enclosed space made it just that much louder. (Matt Avery Photo, Courtesy Mecum Auctions)

Owners Sean Kiernan and his sister Kelly look somewhat anxious as their famous Mustang rolls toward the auction block. It's doubtful John Wayne and Elvis would draw any more attention as they walked down the sidewalk together than this particular spectacle. Mecum was obviously very serious about security for this sure-to-be multi-million-dollar bit of movie Mustang history. Note the cautious-looking armed security guard that walked the car from the display area to the block. The bearded gent poking his head in the passenger-side window to chat with the Kiernans is NBCSN television auction analyst and commentator Steve Machett. (Photo Courtesy Anthony Bologna)

its annual schedule. With well over 3,000 cars that cross the block during auction week, it's the largest single-location collector car auction in the world. Media coverage of the much-anticipated Mustang sale was large and diverse. There was considerable attention paid as to what day of the week and what time of day the car was to be sold. Ultimately, the calculation was made to roll the car across the auction block during the live television broadcast window on Friday afternoon of that week's event.

Sean Kiernan drove the car to and up onto the block and heartily revved the throaty 390 most of the way. His sister Kelly rode shotgun and his wife Samantha walked alongside the car. Sean's mother and daughter also attended the event. The 559 was lot number F150, which stood for Friday, January 10, 2020, Lot 150 for the day—not the Ford truck. The drama and pandemonium that led up to the car taking its place on the block was parsed out for maximum in-room and on-air impact. The Florida arena was packed full with not a single empty seat.

Since the Kiernans paid $3,500 for the 559 *Bullitt* Mustang, as the only responder to an ad in *Road & Track* magazine in 1974, the family felt that number should be the appropriate opening bid for the car in 2020. Needless to say, it opened to a round of applause and immediately climbed like the altimeter on a fighter jet. It passed $1 million within a few seconds, and didn't take long to reach $2.5 million. There was a combination of bidders inside the building and others on the telephone. Company chief Dana Mecum was down on the stage to orchestrate the proceedings, while auctioneer Matt Moravec stood high atop his podium to ensure he had full view of the room and all possible bidders. The bidding slowed after the $2.5 million mark, but quickly enough it crept up to $3 million with the crowd screaming and chanting B-U-L-L-I-T-T the whole time.

By this point, the competition was down to one bidder in the house and another anonymous bidder on the phone with the auction team. Eventually, it crept up to $3.4 million in favor of the phone bidder. The auctioneer gave the bidders in the house plenty of opportunity to bump the bid to $3.5 million, which they declined to do and waved off. The hammer fell for a gavel price of $3.4 million, which is nearly 1,000 times the opening bid. That amount, plus the customary auction buyer's premium commission, equaled $3.74 million total sale price, which is the highest figure ever paid for an American muscle car at public auction. As of this writing, the identity of the winning phone bidder has not been disclosed, but the sale was a pulse-pounding finale to this chapter of the *Bullitt* story.

Talk about a "vroom with a view." This amazing photo was caught just prior to the commencement of bidding. You can see the roof of the Mustang on the block, and the gentleman in the black cowboy hat at the lower right is the auctioneer. (Photo Courtesy Mecum Auctions)

The big screen behind the podium tells much of the story. The car is bid to $3.4 million, and the auctioneer, with hammer held high, is asking for $3.5. Failing any further advance, he declared the car sold at $3.4 million, plus the bidder's premium commission. (David Newhardt Photo Courtesy Mecum Auctions)

Done deal! The sign and numbers tell the rest of the story, as the 559 Bullitt Mustang finds its first new home since 1974. (Photo Courtesy Anthony Bologna)

As if to put a final seal of approval on the historic sale, Dana Mecum himself slaps the traditional "SOLD" sticker to 559's windshield, and thus begins the next chapter in this legendary car's fascinating life. (David Newhardt Photo, Courtesy Mecum Auctions)

Bullitt guru Glen Kalmack has spent much of the last 50 years studying every aspect of *Bullitt*, including and most particularly how the Mustangs were modified and prepped for action. He built and for many years owned what many *Bullitt*eers consider to be the most authentic tribute or replica version of the movie Mustang. Here's his to-do list if you decide to build your own:

- 1968 models, not 1967 (there are many subtle differences)
- 390-4V FE big-block V-8
- Ford 4-speed manual toploader transmission
- 3.00:1 9-inch rear end
- Highland Green Metallic exterior paint
- Koni shock absorbers, front and rear
- Front grille painted matte black
- All exterior badges, front grille spotlights, and pony emblems removed, holes filled
- Clear front windscreen, untinted and without graduated top-tint bar
- Backup lights removed from rear fascia
- Three box-iron stock camera mounts under each side of car
- Recessed early-type rear marker lights; not the surface-mounted units used past 2/15/68 production
- Black leather-covered Shelby GT350/500 steering wheel with four holes in each spoke, not slots
- Shelby GT500 horn button
- Side rockers painted in Highland Green Metallic
- Any painted or tape stripes removed
- Side ornaments painted in body color
- Black deluxe interior trim level
- Tachometer/rev counter instrument cluster
- Woodgrain deluxe trim dashboard
- Circular Mustang logo above glove box door
- Black rear taillight surrounds
- Blacked-out rear taillight fascia panel
- Turned down, vertical edge of trunk panel painted body color
- Pop-open fuel cap center and base painted black
- Rearview mirror fixed to windscreen with left to right dipping option (not up and down)
- Wooden gear knob, likely from Porsche
- Interior ceiling/roof console
- Standard, straight-cut steel tailpipes with no chrome tips
- Round Yankee 503 driver's door mirror painted body color
- No A/C
- No headrests on front seats
- Metal deluxe ornaments remain on seats
- No labels on wheel centers
- Firestone high-performance bias ply tires
- JJZ 109 California license plates, yellow on black color scheme, with recessed YOM sticker placements
- 1968 pink YOM sticker on rear license plate only
- Over-riders/bumper guards on front and rear bumpers
- Radio antenna on rear passenger-side fender
- Turn signal indicator hood
- Two turn signal "idiot lights" on turn signal stem
- Two mid-1960s production American Racing Torq Thrust D wheels front, 15x6
- Two mid-1960s production American Racing Torq Thrust D wheels rear, 15x7
- Wheels spokes and lug nuts painted dull black

NORTHERN CHASE ROUTE AND FILMING LOCATION POINTS OF INTEREST

Scene: Jazz club and restaurant
Location: Coffee Cantata: 2026 Union Street, San Francisco, California

Even though the Golden Gate Bridge isn't directly on the chase route, although not for a lack of trying on the production's part, it remains among the very most iconic identifiers of the city and county of San Francisco. It appears in passing and background scenes of the film countless times. Here, the 559 beauty/hero Bullitt Mustang strikes an elegant pose with the third-generation 2019 Mustang Bullitt. Dark Highland Green has never looked better. (Photo Courtesy Anthony Bologna)

Scene: Serving of habeas corpus writ by Chalmers

Location: Grace Cathedral Episcopal Church: 1100 California Street, San Francisco, California

Grace Cathedral also doesn't appear in the chase scene proper but is the backdrop for a lengthy scene between Chalmers and Captain Bennett and his family. The front entry and staircase complex looked slightly different in 1968 than it does today, but the fabulous structure's architecture is unmistakable.

Even though Bullitt's Mustang didn't appear in front of Grace Cathedral in the film, we stopped there to visit this amazing San Francisco landmark with our 2019 Mustang Bullitt.

Scene: Last part of car chase on Guadalupe Canyon Parkway, ending when the Charger crashes at North Hill Drive

Location: Charger crashes into exploding gas station set approximately corner of Quadalupe Canyon Road and 150 North Hills Drive, Brisbane, California

Scene: Suburban Motel and Murder, then the Thunderbird Hotel

Location: Clarion Hotel: 401 E. Millbrae Avenue, Millbrae, California

B **Scene:** Where Bullitt meets up with the informant to discuss Johnny Ross. The CI is the guy with the strange sideburns and orange lens glasses. The building still exists. However, the business is closed and the property is boarded up.

Location: Enrico's Café: 504 Broadway, San Francisco, California

Scene: Lieutenant Bullitt's apartment
Location: 1153–57 Taylor Street, San Francisco, California

The Bullitt production company rented this entire building for use as Lt. Frank Bullitt's apartment building. This handsome 1968 Mustang GT390 fastback Bullitt tribute machine belongs to Dave Kunz.

Next Page: McQueen and one of the Mustangs on Taylor Street, the sign of the most dangerous and exciting stunts within the chase scene. This is where the Charger and the Mustangs are seen flying through the air and landing and bouncing their way down Taylor Street. Hickman drove the Charger for these sequences, and Bud Ekins was at the wheel of the Mustang for most of it. The hard landings bent their share of suspension components in both cars, and at least one Mustang oil pan was fully sacrificed in the name of great cinematography. (Photo Courtesy ©/™ Warner Bros. Entertainment Inc. [sl9])

Scene: VJ Groceries
Location: 1199 Clay Street, San Francisco, California

What was then VJ's Market at the corner of Taylor and Clay still looks much as it did in 1968. The big difference here is the 2019 Mustang Bullitt. The shop owner commented on how many Steve McQueen and Bullitt fans still remember and visit the little store and look to pound their fists on the metal newspaper dispenser rack just as McQueen did in 1968. Sadly, both are no longer around.

Scene: Chalmers' house
Location: 2700 Vallejo Street, Pacific Heights, San Francisco, California

Scene: Embarcadero Freeway, San Francisco, California
Location: Demolished in 1989 due to the Loma Prieta earthquake damage

Scene: Car chase route
Location: Marina Green, Marina District, San Francisco, California

C **Scene:** The lookalike Johnny Ross visits the hotel to ask the front desk for messages, and also to be seen in the taxi line to put the Mafia on notice that he'd arrived in town.
Location: Mark Hopkins Hotel: 999 California Street, San Francisco, California

Scene: Beginning of the downhill chase scene culminating at Taylor and Filbert streets
Location: Taylor and Vallejo Streets, Russian Hill, San Francisco, California

The car may be a new Mustang Bullitt, but the streets are just as narrow and steep as they were in 1968; all of which reminds us of the extraordinary car control exhibited by McQueen, Loftin, Hickman, and Ekins. At least one parked car and one camera were clipped along the way during three weeks of action-packed driving and filming, but otherwise no one was hurt nor was there any irreparable property damage.

Scene: At the start of the high-speed chase, the cars roar up Chestnut Street, past the San Francisco Art Institute (screen left), and turn south onto Leavenworth Street

Location: 800 block of Chestnut Street, Russian Hill, San Francisco, California

Scene: Cathy runs from the car

Location: Highway 101 (Candlestick Park Exit), San Francisco, California

D **Scene:** The Chicago scene at the beginning of the movie
Location: 450 Sutter Street Garage (450 Sutter Street, San Francisco, California)

The 450 Sutter Street Garage entrance isn't seen in the chase or the film, but this locale was important to the production. During the somewhat shadowy garage sequence during the opening scene setter, the interior was darkened considerably, as Johnny Ross escapes an assassination attempt before fleeing Chicago to San Francisco, where he attempts to leave the country.

Scene: Bullitt tailed by hitmen
Location: Cesar Chavez and York Streets, Mission District, San Francisco, California

Scene: General chase
Location: Columbus and Lombard Streets, North Beach, San Francisco, California

Scene: Hitmen lose sight of Bullitt's car
Location: Intersection of York and Peralta, Bernal Heights, San Francisco, California

Scene: Daniels Hotel. This was the hotel where the stand-in Johnny Ross was being housed pending trial. This is where he was assassinated by the Mafia hitmen and where the SFPD detective who worked for Bullitt was shot in the leg. The building sat along the San Francisco waterfront in view of the Golden Gate bridge, but the building was torn down long ago, and the area now looks completely different.
Location: Kennedy Hotel, 226 Embarcadero, San Francisco, California

Scene: Finale shootout
Location: San Francisco International Airport

Scene: San Francisco Police Department (SFPD) headquarters
Location: 850 Bryant Street, San Francisco, California

Scene: San Francisco General Hospital Medical Center
Location: 1001 Potrero Avenue, Potrero Hill, San Francisco, California

Scene: General chase
Location: 20th and Vermont streets, Potrero Hill, San Francisco, California

Scene: Miscellaneous pick-up shots (villain fastens seat belt)
Location: Warner Brothers Burbank Studios: 4000 Warner Boulevard, Burbank, California

Scene: Bimbo's 365 Cabaret
Location: 1025 Columbus Avenue, San Francisco, California

Bimbo's cabaret is still in business and hosts many frontline acts. In spite of its modest façade, it's old school and has a very elegant cabaret room inside. It's also available for group events and party rentals. Frank Sinatra, the Grateful Dead, and David Bowie all performed there. This location is highly significant to the film and the chase scene, as it's just about here that the first burnouts take place and the high-speed aspect of the chase begins.

Scene: High-speed passages in the chase scene down by the water front
Location: Bayshore Boulevard near Cesar Chavez, Bayview, San Francisco, California

Scene: General location reference of some of chase scene
Location: Fillmore Street, Russian Hill, San Francisco, California

Scene: General location reference of some of chase scene
Location: John Muir Drive, Lake Merced, San Francisco, California

Scene: The Mustang's famous reverse-gear burnout scene (also where Charger clips and destroys one film camera)
Location: Larkin and Chestnut streets, Russian Hill, San Francisco, California

This all-important intersection is home to several significant events in the filming of the chase. Primarily it's the spot where McQueen as Bullitt misses a complex set of right turns at high speed, which is often attributed to a truck that may have been backing out into the roadway, then executes the famous reverse gear, wheel-hopping burnout, prior to righting the direction of the car and peeling off in pursuit of the Charger. In a different angle of the same spot at a different moment in the chase, the Charger also runs wide of the turn and takes out a stationary camera. We'll admit that having the 2019 Mustang Bullitt in this location made us desperately want to replicate the reverse burnout, and we only wish we could have told you that we did.

Scene: A sweeping downhill lefthander where the Charger bangs the wall and loses at least one more hubcap; view of San Francisco Bay and Alcatraz
Location: Larkin and Francisco streets, Russian Hill, San Francisco, California

This is right at the point at Francisco and Larkin Streets where the Charger takes out a stationary camera positioned just to the Charger's left as mentioned above. The car was fishtailing mightily, and due to his great skill and perhaps a bit of luck, Hickman kept the car from doing further damage to itself or other cars parked on the street. This isn't an actual scene from the film, but is a bit of recreation using Frank A. Panacci's superb movie car tribute Charger. (Photo Courtesy of Anthony Bologna)

Among the most scenic overlooks on the chase scene, and some would say in the entire film, is the curvy downhill intersection of Larkin and Francisco streets. Both the Mustang and Charger cross this intersection, and the Charger clips the stub wall on the right side of the curve and loses yet another hubcap.

Scene: Taylor Street: where most of the Mustang and Charger jump scenes occurred
Location: Russian Hill, San Francisco, California. Cars head up and down Taylor Street between approximately Broadway and Filbert.

Scene: San Francisco-Oakland Bay Bridge
Location: San Francisco Bay, California

Scene: Hitmen begin to trail Bullitt
Location: Cesar Chavez Street and Potrero Avenue, San Francisco, California

Scene: Car chase begins. A ramp was constructed on 20th Street to make Mustang jump onto Rhode Island Street.
Location: 20th Street from Rhode Island Street to Kansas Street, San Francisco, California

Scene: Final car chase montage
Location: Guadalupe Parkway, Daly City, California

So much happened in or near the Little Italy section of San Francisco, more properly called North Beach. Somehow the modern version of Lt. Bullitt's car looks very at home on these streets, many of which have changed relatively little since 1968.

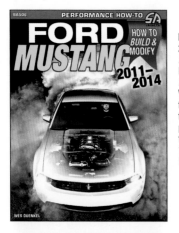
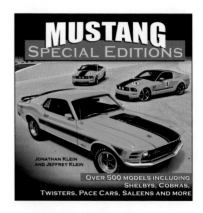
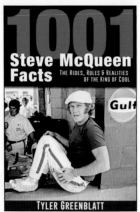

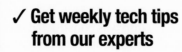

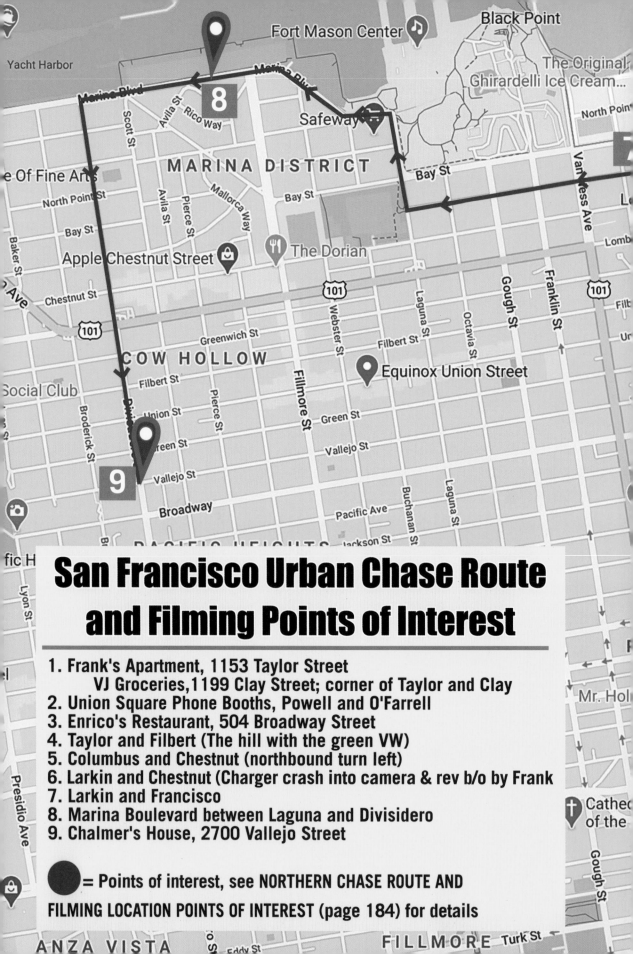

San Francisco Urban Chase Route and Filming Points of Interest

1. Frank's Apartment, 1153 Taylor Street
   VJ Groceries, 1199 Clay Street; corner of Taylor and Clay
2. Union Square Phone Booths, Powell and O'Farrell
3. Enrico's Restaurant, 504 Broadway Street
4. Taylor and Filbert (The hill with the green VW)
5. Columbus and Chestnut (northbound turn left)
6. Larkin and Chestnut (Charger crash into camera & rev b/o by Frank
7. Larkin and Francisco
8. Marina Boulevard between Laguna and Divisidero
9. Chalmer's House, 2700 Vallejo Street

⬤ = Points of interest, see NORTHERN CHASE ROUTE AND

FILMING LOCATION POINTS OF INTEREST (page 184) for details